The God
of
Zebidar

The God
of
Zebidar

GOD IS IMMANENT

Merid Tadesse Ergicho

Editing, Design, typesetting and publishing by UK Book Publishing
www.ukbookpublishing.com

Cover Photo Credit – Sebesibe Tadesse Ergicho

ISBN: 978-1-916572-77-5

A NOTE FROM THE AUTHOR

In the loving memory of my dad,
Tadesse Ergicho Fule Dendiso.

My dad used to say, "It is better to do a smaller amount of work than talk more." He was practical – a gentleman who stands by his word. In his retirement, he changed the entire back garden with sugarcane plants and later with a different type of herb called "Gesho" which could be commercialised to ferment local beverages called "Tejj" and "Tela". He applied crop rotation to manage pest infestations, to prevent plant diseases and keep the soil healthy.

He encouraged his children to study hard all the time. He also enhanced students in the community by buying a pack of Bic pens and giving them to individual students. He believes that education gives choices in life. He was phenomenal! Every single pen, pencil and stationeries I see wasted on the floors in the different schools I worked in the UK reminded me of my father and how thoughtful he was. People have taken so many things for granted here.

One of the most important things my dad instructed and taught me in my life was to respect authority. *"Fear the Lord and the king, my son, and do not join with rebellious officials."* (Proverbs 24:21) One day, I was talking about my primary school friends with my younger brother, Sebesibe. Hence, I mentioned one of them by name, Mengistu, to explain what had happened in school. By coincidence, that name also happened to be the name of the President of Ethiopia at that time – Lt. Colonel Mengistu Haile Mariam. My dad thought I was mentioning the President's name and making fun of him. He reacted with a speed of light to unbuckle his trousers' leather belt from his waist to discipline me. "How dare you call the President's name?" he shouted at me. Before I gave him a reply that I was not talking about the President, I had already received my punishment of whipping. I still sometimes laugh with that lovely memory of the living room at my home in Butajira, Ethiopia.

I like to think, hope and believe my father is in his heavenly home. He was miraculously saved and received Lord Jesus Christ as his personal saviour.

This book is for him.

ABOUT THE AUTHOR

Merid is a born-again Christian and street evangelist. He has one beautiful wife and two ever-loving daughters.

He pursued his Master's Degree in Development Studies from London South Bank University (LSBU), a Postgraduate Diploma in Education from the Institute of Education, University College London (UCL) and a Bachelor Degree in Political Science and International Relations (PSIR) from the Social Science Colleges, Addis Ababa University.

Professionally, he has been an educator in Further Education Colleges in London and is currently working in a High School in Croydon.

He is a Zebilon (Zebidar-London) Author. Zebilon is a future trademark or brand of books written by our family members.

His nephew, Josh (Eyasu) Ashenafi Biratu showed interest in joining the group and he will be leading ZebiTex (Zebidar-Texas). branch.

And also, his nieces Dr Eden Ayele Biltibo and Dr Lidiya Ayele Biltibo are joining the group by publishing their general medical practices and they earn their titles of ZebiTen (Zebidar-Tenessee) and ZebiTon (Zebidar-Galveston) respectively.

He met the late Queen Elizabeth II for a couple of times whilst he was working as a diplomat in the Ethiopian Embassy, London, during which time he had opportunities to briefly talk to Her Majesty.

What was in his conversation with the Queen is revealed in this book.

I hope you enjoy the book.

ACKNOWLEDGEMENTS

My deepest reverence goes to my Heavenly Father Who is good all the time.

I would like to express my gratitude to my brilliant wife, Mrs Bizuaeyehu and to my Crystal Black Diamond daughters Abigail & Joanna for whom I have endless love.

My mum, Mrs Worknesh Woldemariam Melsebo, you are so good at loving people and you taught me how to be kind. I deeply appreciate the sacrifices that you have made as a mother. No matter what life throws at you, remember that I'll always be by your side—just like you've been there for me. You deserve the best things in life and I will fervently pray for you that Sovereign and Supreme God remembers you for something good. You are the kind of mum everyone wishes they had and kindness is one of your greatest characteristics. You are my role model. Long live my magnanimous mother!

My siblings, six sisters namely Wosene (Ehtemete), Amarech (Ehitabeba), Wolela, Hiywot, Tsion and Kebebush – thank you for being my lovely sisters. By the same token, my six brothers – Bruk (Wondimtila), Endeshaw, Tariku, Sileshi, Mesfin and Sebesibe – my thanks go to each one of you for being my brave brothers. Family is a gift from God, so is life. Live longer and enjoy life at its best with good health!

I would like to travel to Gondar and explore more, especially the seven mountains around the city of Gondar – Mushra Dengay, Achenakir, Maldiba, Aman Anba, Sanita Anba, Enchduba and Maraki Anba.

I am eternally grateful to Ruth Lunn for copy editing, Judith Barker for project management, and Jay Thompson for the design of the book.

I would also like to extend my deepest gratitude to my friend, Dr Ali, for his invaluable comments on the final edition of the book.

CONTENTS

CHAPTER 1

I am from
ZEBIDAR!

Climb up to the summit of ZEBIDAR – the Proud Chains of Mountains in Butajira, a small town in the Southern Region of Ethiopia and you will tell me if you ever forget the experience, for I know I have not.

The first time I committed myself to talking about ZEBIDAR was in 1993, twenty years after I was born. I was in my third year of Social Science Studies of Political Science and International Relations (PSIR) at Addis Ababa University. I am proud that I belong to Zebidar – Majestic Chains of Love Mountains!

It was my turn to present a lecture on a coursework for Local Administration Course. The course was supervised by a very respected professor named Dr Yacob Arsano Atito. My memory is still fresh – as he taught his courses without showing any personal bias towards what he was teaching. He was a competent and professional lecturer. Thank you so much, Dr Yacob Arsano Atito!

On my micro teaching lecture, Dr Mekonnen Disasa, from the Institute of Language Studies (ILS), (Foreign Language Department – English) was invited to attend. At that time, he was conducting research about the ability of university students on their 'Spoken English'.

I opened my energetic lecture to my department students remarking, "This is the best original kitfo-lecture on Region Seven you will probably ever have in your lifetime." And it was! My political psychology prediction was right as I said it was an outstanding lecture on the region as region 7 (Guraghe Region) ceased to exist when five regions merged together to form the Southern Regional Administration.

It was a perfect warm up! I went into the details. It was a hot lecture by any standard, full of a wealth of information and persuading arguments as my research was based on primary data and I had also interviewed several very prominent political figures in the region – it was information directly from the horse's mouth. My audience was fully absorbed.

As soon as I had finished and thanked my audience for listening attentively and intently, Dr Mekonnen Disasa came towards me with a smile on his face to congratulate and praise my efforts. He asked, "Are you from St Joseph School (a prestigious school in the capital city, Addis Ababa)?"

I proudly answered, "No, I am not. I AM FROM ZEBIDAR. (ZEBIDAR was my Trademark Brand.) I am from Butajira." He looked puzzled that either his educated guess was not right or perhaps he did not know the whereabouts of my hometown and I could read a real excitement on his face that a guy from the countryside was able to present such an eloquent lecture with an air of confidence.

To the surprise of most of my university friends, who assumed that I was from Addis, they also learned that day that I was from Butajira, a great town which is blessed by God in possession of ZEBIDAR, the Whispering Chains of Mountains. Zebidar Mountain Chains are rows of high mountain summits, a linear sequence of interconnected or related mountains, or a contiguous ridge of mountains within a larger mountain range. From high up on the summit of the mountain, they had a spectacular view of green meadows and streams like silver ribbons.

As it happens, I graduated from Addis Ababa University in July 1994 and it was time for me to look for a job for my living. Every PSIR graduates' dream was to join the Ministry of Foreign Affairs of Ethiopia and eventually to serve her/his country as a diplomat. However, at the time there was no vacancy posted in Addis Zemen newspaper – a tabloid newspaper in Ethiopia. We needed to wait for some time.

Some of my university friends informed me that different regions were employing PSIR graduates as history teachers as there was a shortage of that particular department graduates to teach in high schools. I decided to go to my regional office's Central Public Authority (CPA) and register for future opportunities to be a history teacher. So, I have to travel to Hawassa, the capital city of the Southern Peoples' Administrative Region.

I was on board in a passenger bus two days before the Ethiopian New Year 1987 (1994 in the Gregorian calendar), seated in the middle of two complete strangers, one young, similar to my age and the other a bit older. Religiously speaking, the one who was seated on my left, Mr Bekele, was in the protestant denomination like me, and on my right, Mr Wasihun was a Muslim. I was engaging both of them with different topics about nature and life – I could tell both liked me and I was glad that I made a great impression on them.

The driver of the bus announced that he would not be driving to Hawassa as it was getting late in the evening and passengers who were destined to go to Hawassa were advised to come early in the morning at 6am. The town for sleepover was Shashemene and I had never been there before. Luckily, both Bekele and Wasihun were from this town and I was cordially invited to spend the night over in either of their homes.

A time had come for me to decide and I chose to go to Mr Wasihun's family home. He had one wife and two young children at the time. He owned a big furniture shop on the street. He owned a good villa as well. I was served with dinner and allocated a bedroom for the night. He told me that he had a sister in Hawassa who owned a restaurant and promised to call her and my lunch would be waiting for me after I finished my business. He told me his personal details once I decided to stay the night over with him and his family.

In the morning he took me to the bus station. After a big "Thank you!" hug, I was on board to my final destination – Hawassa. This was God's grace and favour on me to be looked after by a stranger that I would not be too much disappointed by an officer who was like a snake in the grass.

It was not difficult to get the CPA Office of the Region as I asked a gentleman on the street for directions and he tipped me how to get there. What was not straightforward was to convince the unfriendly officer who was in charge of registering who would be history teachers for future openings in some schools of the region. He enquired why I had come there and I informed him that I would like to be registered as a history teacher. Right there he started to mock me!

He said, "You PSIR students – were you not the ones who were telling us that you will be diplomats and carried briefcases when we were at the university? Look at you now, you carried your educational documents in a plastic bag and are begging me to register you to be a history teacher." That was not what I expected from someone in a public office. He roared, "You have incurred unnecessary costs travelling all the way from Addis Ababa to Hawassa on the eve of New Year for something which I would not offer you."

He commented that he remembered me on Campus as I was one junior in joining the university. However, I used to have many friends in the senior years with whom I used to hang out. It could be because Addis Ababa University was not my first university after all. I was at Asmara University studying Chemistry major with minor Geology.

I needed to change my field of study for I had known I had set my heart on being a diplomat. I am a natural communicator at any level – personal or government affairs. I had been in so many professional medical doctors' briefings at Asmara Hospital with my cousin who was a dentist, Dr Mengistu Yilma. Thank you, Dr Mengistu, for the exposure and experience you brought into my life! May God bless you and your family for eternity!

The General Director of the hospital in Asmara who studied Veterinary Doctorate and worked as a Vet for some years knew this profession was not his. He joined to study Medical Science afresh and successfully finished his MD and then he was living his dreams. He was so knowledgeable, competent in his work as a General Director. He tipped me with his best advice – if you are not happy with what you are doing now – change it. The earlier the better! He opened up my intellectual eyes!

I did also remember this officer in the CPA Office Hawassa from a distance whilst we were in the university likewise. He had taken some of the department jokes by students seriously. We used to say, ILS stands for "International Lazy Students" whereas it meant "International Language Studies". Sociology graduates end up with their mules for transportation in the countryside as there may not be any roads for cars, PSIR students will be future diplomats, presidents and prime ministers.

Moreover, Law graduates will be Little Matlock (from American mystery legal drama *television series* created by Dean Hargrove, starring Andy Griffith in the title role of criminal defence *attorney . . .*) or lions in courts and flies outside, Economics graduates knows how to manage other people's money but they won't have any for themselves, Accountants are hot-cakes (they were getting employment even before they finish their studies), etc. I guess he suffered from inferiority complex instead of enjoying the jokes as they were meant to be for fun.

Anyway, I wished he had taken the photocopies of my application at that moment, and torn them up unseen and thrown them into the waste paper basket as soon as I left his office. He did not mind about my feelings and wellbeing – he was so cruel! You'd be surprised, but there are people like him with poor judgement everywhere on our big, beautiful earth. We should try our best to make them better people if any opportunity arises, and also pray for them. If I could not forgive them, how could it be possible for me to be genuinely praying, "*The Lord's Prayer?*" ". . . and forgive us our trespasses as we forgive those who trespass against us . . ."

He said, "Good-bye!" Adios!

Then it was my turn to tell him before leaving his office which he did not deserve to run for lack of professionalism, good manners and work etiquette as a public servant. I bragged, "Sir, for your information, there is nothing as such called 'unnecessary cost' in Political Science. Every step I had taken to come over to this office was necessary though you were not helpful." At least I learned that there are some uncooperative and unhelpful people on this big, beautiful earth. I left this vile man's office.

Then, my mind was instantly racing about the promise Wasihun had made the previous evening. I love food and I thanked God that He let me encounter an angel, Wasihun, on my journey for my first job hunt which was not successful. Nonetheless, with hindsight I could see now it was not successful for a reason. God did not want me to miss the job He had prepared for me by going afar where I could not be traced or where I could not follow up the vacancies advertised by the Foreign Office. He did not want me to miss His perfect plan and purpose in my life – serve Foreign Ministry for some time and evangelise in the streets of London and bring lost lives into His Kingdom.

Right away, I started to search for "Zenbaba Hotel and restaurant" which belongs to Wasihun's sister. Hallelujah! I found it! Wasihun's sister was as generous as her brother. She gave me the most beautiful, big smile as I introduced myself to her. She told me that her brother had already called her to inform her that I was coming for lunch. She gave me a royal welcome with a red-carpet treatment! Thank you ever so much, Wasihun and your sister for your unreserved generosity you had shown to someone whom you even did not know. Regrettably, I did not tell you about the most precious treasure in life – belonging to the Lord Jesus Christ. He is the LORD of Lords. Will there be any chance for you to find this book and read it? I do not know. But, one thing I know – God loves you too much and finds a way to welcome you to His Kingdom.

All the special meals, hot and cold canapes, roasted lamb, vegetables and juices were on my table and I was served like a king. The treatment was extraordinary. I was starving! The officer had doubled or tripled my food appetite and I thanked her and devoured all the food. I always had an excellent appetite, whether I am ill or in good health. It is a gift from God. I might be tempted to ask for a meal when I go to my heavenly home – but there will be no food. Will I ever miss it? No, I won't as I will be in a different realm! There is nothing in this universe as beautiful and satisfying as the presence of God.

I have a friend who is a multi-millionaire but does not enjoy food as much as I do. This world we are living in could sometimes be mysterious. The people who had the money may not have a good stomach and the people who had a wholesome appetite may not have enough food to enjoy as much as they wanted. But for me, in my university years, I had one day which I used to call "Food Day!". As soon as I received fifty Ethiopian Birr, I would go to three or four different restaurants in a row and celebrate my student pocket money which was given to me from my dad and big brother Bruk. Thank you, my dad, and thank you, Bruk. You are blessed like your name and enjoy life at its best with your family.

Any remaining money after I spent on my food programme of the month would be budgeted to buy bars of soaps to wash my clothes.

Anyway, I did not have lots of clothes and hence I could still lend some money to my borrowers. Especially to Mr Mekonnen Alehegne who sold an ox and was in possession of over seven hundred Ethiopian Birr at that time. This was an equivalent amount to one hundred US dollars. He could have been a student investor at the time with all that money if he knew what to do with it. He loved to borrow from me for a bus ticket – fifteen cents.

The way he used to address me was, "Dr Merid, My World Bank, could you lend me one Ethiopian Birr?" How could I say "No" to him? He was too polite and I would always love to lend to him. I did not mind that he had a lot of money and also I was not so sure whether he returned my borrowed money or not. Moreover, I used to buy two of my best friends Coca-Cola and Pepsi every time I received my monthly pocket money. I guess, I was very generous as a university student.

He used to bring arake/katikala – a strong alcoholic beverage which was fermented locally in various parts of Ethiopia. I had never drunk but people say Dembecha's arake was one of the best in the land. He offered me a try several times but I did not welcome his invitation.

Mr Merid dealing with other diplomats.

The first time I ever tried wine was when I was working as a diplomat in London, in the UK. My embassy hosted a National Day celebration every year, and I was approached by my boss, the Ambassador. He said, "Mr Merid, you need to start drinking wine to socialise. You invite other people from the Foreign Office, Home Office, Commerce Office, British Members of Parliament, investors, etc and that you were not drinking wine may not be most welcoming to them." That is how people could manipulate you to destroy your life – a long good habit of not drinking alcohol as a core value. They will try to rationalise drinking alcohol as part of your work or socialisation. No, it is not!

He joked, "The soldiers serve their country with their lives, diplomats serve their country with their livers." I might have drunk half a cup of wine but stopped when I changed my career from diplomacy to teaching as my eldest daughter, Abigail, reminded me that I am the Temple of Holy Spirit and I should not pollute my body with alcoholic drinks. May the Lord Jesus Christ richly bless you, my dearest Abigail, in your choice of medicine as your future career.

"Do you not know that your bodies are temples of the Holy Spirit, who is in you, whom you have received from God? You are not your own; you were bought at a price. Therefore, honour God with your bodies." (1 Corinthians 6: 19-20)

CHAPTER 2

Zebidar Roars!

"Before the mountains were born or you brought forth the whole world, from everlasting to everlasting you are God." (Psalm 90:2)

Suddenly there was a cry from my soul! It was a memory of my hometown, Butajira. Zebidar is a long soaring chain of majestic mountains which surround the town of Butajira. My beautiful hometown!

Ages ago, I climbed up to the summit of Zebidar. I couldn't forget the spectacular view of green meadows and streams like silver ribbons. Split, cracked and carved by the magic of nature, the rocks had created a path of shimmering pillars and arches.

African, European, Asian, Australian, Canadian and American bikers and mountain climbers should be advised and encouraged to tour Ethiopia and sample the glorious chains of mountains for single-track or path mountain bikes and mountain climbing. Furthermore, the steep path glistened with damp – polished by nature into dangerous slippery slopes – is ideal for adventure tourism.

There is more to offer for nature lovers in this great town of Butajira, the home of the brave. The majestic trees stand tall and proud. The trees are joined together like a crowd of vivid green umbrellas. The magnificent trees fling their branches up to the sun to frame the deep blue sky. This is true for the most part of the Southern Peoples' Administrative Region including Butajira.

Consider one of the West African countries – Sierra Leone. The name "Sierra Leone" is adapted from the Portuguese language. It means "Lion Mountain". "Why Lion Mountain?" I asked to some of my Sierra Leonese friends. They told me it was because when the wind howls against the mountains – it roars like a lion!

In retrospect, whilst I was in my Junior Secondary School, as I woke up early in the morning for my studies, I used to hear various sounds. One of them was caused by large trucks far off in the distance moving along the main road of Butajira. You could guess they were moving very slowly from the sounds they made. I wondered whether our lives were as slow as the big trucks passing by either direction of Butajira.

The most beautiful, serene and soft sounds created by our two main rivers, namely Erenzaf and Eresha, our finest spring water of the highest quality which could be bottled and used locally as well as exported for international commerce to earn foreign exchange were extraordinary. The spring water which flew calm and smooth as silk was located behind St Mary Church.

Moreover, the sounds which came from Hara Sheitan Volcanic Lake of Butajira was as quiet and soft as velvet. The aforementioned physical sounds were clearly heard with physical ears by anyone who wakes up early in the morning. What was unique and extraordinary was the voice which came from Zebidar Chains of Mountains. Like the mountains in Sierra Leone, Zebidar ROARS! Wait, even more alarming, they were/are Whispering Mountains if you listen to them closely with spiritual ears. They whisper among one another saying, "Jesus is the LORD!" You need to develop the sixth sense organ to witness this!

Zebidar, Chains of Mountains, whisper also, "Children of Butajira, my children, ask not what your country can do for you, ask what you can do for your country." The Guraghe Chains of Mountains, Zebidar had said this famous saying even a long time before John F. Kennedy, the 35th president of the United States of America. Zebidar whispered it thousands of years ago.

On the flip side of not taking a good note of Zebidar's pieces of advice, I did not forget several incidents which happened in my youth. Once, friends of mine and I from the village decided to break into a farm and took some peas and bean seeds for eating. I joined the small village gang to steal.

We went over to a place called "Netsa sefer" meaning "Freedom Village". It was a bit of a distance away, at the back of Saint Mary, Butajira's Orthodox Church. We were about seven or eight of us. Without a good strategy of theft and observation, we jumped into the farm. None of us noticed the farmer who owned the farm was there removing the weeds from his cultivation.

He probably did not think in his wildest imagination that there would be an army of small kids (human weeds) in daylight destroying his produce. Like a flash of thunderstorm, he came running towards us having his spear in his right hand to scare us though I did not know his real intentions. All of my friends ran away in the same direction to where we had come from except me who had run a different way, taking a slight left into the jungle.

I made a wrong turn and choice to escape from the farmer and he chose to run after me – the weakest link. He must have known I would not go any further because right after the jungle was a steep gorge and if I jumped into it, I could not survive. Thus, I was held as a captive of theft in his farm, representing the small village gang. The farmer held one of my arms and started to pick some ears of maize from his farm. Mind you, I was not even stealing maize but peas and beans. They were different types of plants.

Perhaps, his intention was that it was easier for me to carry them on my shoulders as the children and people on the street would be chanting, "Thief! Flog him! Thief! Thief! Whip him!" as I walked through the streets of my hometown naming and shaming me. That might have been his good plan! As you well know, a thief had no right to argue with a farmer to say, "I did not take the maize but peas and beans!" It did not matter. I was arrested for stealing on someone's property. I was a thief! It was a very eerie and painful experience as a Grade 5 student in a Primary School.

Behold! Something unexpected was happening. Two boys whom I knew in my school who were in the same Grade suddenly showed up and told the farmer not to proceed with his plan of naming and shaming me as a thief, which I deserved at the time.

I could hear them telling the farmer that I was a very bright student academically in my class and that the incident must have been a one-off as I had never been involved in such kind of criminal activities. They were saying, "This boy, Merid, is an innocent boy. Moreover," they added, "you would be in trouble and regret your actions later as his father is a district judge – a famous one and will retaliate for defaming him and his family! Release him – let him go free!" My angels in times of troubles! Thank you, Midow and Serwana.

The farmer came to me and said, "Go in peace, lad! You do not deserve this. I had known enough about you and your family but never involve yourself in such kind of illegal activities in the future." I was sent home free and by the time I reached "Selam Sefer" meaning "Peaceful Village" my friends were there waiting for me and asked me what had happened.

I told them the whole story from A to Z. I learned my life-lesson at an early age which served me as a good foundation for the rest of my life. A stepping stone which helped me develop my core values and high integrity in my future life. Lots of temptations were coming my way but I have never compromised with my motto of "Honesty is the best policy". Honesty is the cornerstone of my life. Is it for you? I am asking YOU.

Honesty, honour, integrity and probity are great qualities of a personality. Honesty implies a refusal to lie, steal, or deceive in any way. Honour suggests an active or anxious regard for the standards of one's profession, calling, or position. In simple terms, integrity is having strong moral principles based on honesty and to follow those principles religiously while the fourth element – probity – is more from the professional point of view, being non corrupt, fair, upright character or action etc.

In the Literacy campaign for adult education, there were five boys including me and five girls of the same year except our leader who was a voluntary campaigner and much older than the rest of us. One time a dispute arose and he physically assaulted one of the female campaigners. He slapped her on the face and the mark of his fingerprints were there on her skin visible when she came and showed me. Speechless with rage, I curled my fist and dug my fingers deep into my palms. I wanted to show her that I was very angry with what he had done to her.

That she came to me first was because we were close friends in the campaign. It was a challenge for me as she was showing me the giant fingerprint on her face and telling me of his extreme cruelty. I could read her eyes pleading to me saying, "Will you die if I ask you to die? Will you fight Goliath on my behalf and slain for me?" Her father and my father were good friends as well – RIP both! I hope they will meet in Heaven and remember some of their earthly good lives. Will they?

Could you fight for me? I wished I could but did not have the courage at that time. My heart was heavy on him for his brutality, but fighting him could have been very challenging for me. His red eyes burning with a cruel light from his long, snarling face were terrifying. Rumours say once he broke into someone's farm to steal a khat. When the farm owner came to check his farm, this guy immediately took off all his clothes unseen and started to wave his hands sideways, jump up and down and run towards the owner. The owner thinking, he was a demonic force appearing physically ran away from his own property to save his life, saying words of quick prayers "Besime ab, Wewold, Wemenifes Kidus" meaning "Of the Father, of the Son and of the Holy Spirit!" Satan go away!

This was the kind of man I was facing with a very bad reputation. Rumours also said that he had previously broken into a female campaigner's home in Deloach (a small town 48 kilometres away from Butajira). Thus, I took her to the rest of the male campaigners and all of us were very upset by his wrongdoing. Anonymously, we agreed to charge him to the district administration. We wrote statements to file a case as they were but his past wrongdoings which were ignored in good times were also included. Justice would prevail!

One most dreadful evening for me was the night when one of the male literacy campaigners got his knife from his mattress to stab or slaughter the leader for what he had done to this innocent young lady. An attack on a vulnerable member of the literacy campaign could be taken as an attack on another member. Thus, taking justice into one's own hand on behalf of the heart-broken and distressed would be considered as heroic action. But, did his action make the situation any better? Matters did not turn tragic to the level of losing someone's life among us as we cried for help. The chairman of the farmers' association, his deputy and other neighbours came for help. It was decided that the leader of the

Literacy Campaign would stay the night in the chairman's home and the other member who was fighting in the deputy chair's home. Soon after, the district administrator accompanied by two other officers came from Butajira to see the literacy centre and judge over the outstanding case which was filed against the Literacy Campaign leader.

The case was presented by one of the boys whom we nominated to represent us. After the statements were read, the defendant was asked if there were any false accusations. One of the allegations read as, "He forcefully broke into the female campaigners' home." I recall in one instance one of the young ladies did not sleep the whole night as she did not feel safe. She filled gasoline to the brim of the lantern and stayed awake reading a fiction book entitled "Yaltekefele Eda", meaning 'Unpaid Debt' by an Ethiopian authors. She was guarding the rest of the girls who were sleeping from potential forceful sexual harassment.

The leader of the literacy campaign (the defendant) said that there was one thing he wanted to add, that he was not the only male campaigner who was sleeping in the female campaigners' home. He pointed out "Merid also used to sleep in their house which belongs to the female campaigners more times than me".

The district administrator looked at me and asked if what was being said was right.

I answered, "Yes, I sometimes would go for a sleepover to the young ladies' house. But my case was different from his." I explained: "Whenever we had male visitors from somewhere else, the young ladies would say, 'We would like to take Merid so that you could have more space'. Every single one of the young lady campaigners were happy about me joining them – it was a consented one. I always slept in the middle of two best friends who wanted to share their mattresses with me. The victim (plaintiff) was the one who

17

used to give me her arm as my pillow and our legs lying crossed one on the top of the other and we slept peacefully. We trusted each other with kindness, understanding, patience and courtesy. We dictate where the ship sails – not the wind."

Eventually, the leader was dismissed with strong recommendations not to be seen in the literacy centre for whatsoever reason. If he was seen within a twenty kilometres radius around the centre, he would be sent to prison. Protection was guaranteed by the district administration authorities. Then there was some reshuffling of work due to the removal of the leader from the campaign. I was assigned as the new Chairman of Food Committee for a couple of months in the Literacy Campaign, effective the day the leader was dismissed.

One of the other three young men took the leadership role. Our income was provided in kind like ten quintals of teff (Ethiopian herb), some corn and vegetables from the farmers for ten (after removal of the leader there were nine of the literacy campaigners in that small farm district called Shershera Bido). As a Food Committee Chairman, I would sell some of the items in the open market in Kela (name of a small town) or Butajira and consume the rest in one month. I would distribute equally among us the remaining money as pocket money – roughly one hundred and twenty Ethiopian Birr for everyone for a couple of months.

The previous Chairman of the Food Committee was in deficit of our food budget let alone giving pocket money to us as he was corrupt. Hence, he was forced to resign in the new structure. He used to have a bad habit of binge-drinking alcohol and chewing khat addiction. Later, everybody knew that there was some financial scandal before and praised me for what I had done. One of our campaigners was saying, "Even though we put Merid in the swamps of money, he could not help himself." He was suggesting that I refused to steal. Guess who this guy was? Our previous chairman of the food committee. I had learnt my lesson from the farm theft at a very young age!

"A good name is better than precious ointment . . ." (Ecclesiastes 7: 1)

When I was working in the Ministry of Foreign Affairs of Ethiopia, something unexpected happened. A local member of staff from an Embassy came to my office in the airport. I welcomed him warmly and invited him to sit on one of the chairs in the office. I asked him if there was anything I could help with, thinking he might need access to the VIP Lounge or some access in other restricted areas of the airport. In stark contrast to that, he cleared his throat and said, "Mr Merid, I had one request from my Embassy for you to take part. If you help us to smuggle our ambassador's briefcase into a commercial plane unchecked when he travels, my Embassy would reward you with $10,000 US Dollars. I hope this task would not be that difficult for you to handle."

Anyway, after listening to what he had to say, I busted into my righteous wrath.

"How dare you talk to me like that!" I roared. Moreover, I added, "Was it because I was kind, friendly and approachable to you? You are asking for something illegal, illogical, insensible and unreasonable . . ." I was shouting at the top of my voice and my body was shivering because of extreme anger . . . I had never had that kind of experience to date. I was on fire burning – my flames were scorching hot. I also could not forget the terrified expression on his face. His teeth jutted out like fangs and curved down over his lower lip in fear. His fear was an electric shock pumping, shivering waves tearing through his body and making his hair stand on end. He apologised and ran away out of my office to the unknown. He had better run before I called an airport police or security!

Run, run, run and never come back.

"If your brother sins, go and show him his fault in private; if he listens to you, you have won your brother." (Matthew 18:15)

I knew I had the authority and trust from the airport immigration, customs, police, security, intelligence, airlines and civil aviation offices. For me, breaching the code of work ethics and integrity was unthinkable after that unforgettable incident in my childhood. Furthermore, I also grew up in an environment where my mum used to advise my dad every single day in the evening when he was working as a district judge in Butajira. After she had asked him how his day had been, she would say, "Gerad (a respectful title to address my dad), if clients ever invited you for soft drinks in a bar they would expect you to twist justice in their favour in the court. Beware you were being bribed for potential corruption."

He had always taken her pieces of advice to his heart as he had witnessed it was working best in his thirty-five years of career. He knew she was advising him from the Living Word of God. She invested a whole lot of her time reading the Bible – her constitution. There was no free lunch without some expectation of twist on my dad's sound and impartial judgement as a judge. How could I forget my mom's nuggets of wisdom and golden principles of life? I had them in the tablets of my heart since then and for eternity.

"Timely advice is lovely, like golden apples in a silver basket." (Proverbs 25:11). To one who listens valid criticism is like a gold earring or other gold jewellery.

There was no way for me to abuse my authority and breach the codes of work ethics at any level with the solid background I had. Imagine what could be inside the briefcase for which I was offered $10,000 US Dollars by the Embassy in Addis Ababa? Could the content be Ethiopia's precious stones like diamond, uranium? Or else, could it be a bomb to destroy the Ethiopian Airlines flight akin the Lockerbie bomb? Pan Am flight 103, also called the Lockerbie bombing, flight of a passenger airliner operated by Pan American World Airways (Pan Am) that exploded over Lockerbie, Scotland, on December 21, 1988, after a bomb was detonated. All 259 people on board were killed, and 11 individuals on the ground also died. Whatever it was, as a junior member of staff, I fought for my country's national interest by fighting corruption at a personal level.

Let me only this time call myself, "One of the untold heroes of Ethiopia from Zebidar, Butajira." I am proud of myself with the way of the King of kings shaping and moulding me. It is an ongoing process – I am not yet there.

"Whoever can be trusted with very little can also be trusted with much, and whoever is dishonest with very little will also be dishonest with much. (Luke 16:10)

The third incident was another annoying and disappointing experience in my work life in the Ministry of Foreign Affairs of Ethiopia. A young airport customs officer kept on requesting to have a drink with me. I never had the time for recreation as my job was a very demanding one and I must be available for any emergency work at any time. That was why I was supplied with a driver, mobile phone and a Motorola.

Stand by 24/7.

Anyway one sunny day in summer it was destined to be our

meeting for a drink. We met at the restaurant where we had arranged, and he offered me a black level whisky which I declined because I had never drunk alcohol in my life. He ordered his choice of an alcoholic drink and I had my Pepsi and started to chat.

He said, "Mr Merid, we knew that you had the authority to command Airport Customs Office for items which belong to guests of the Prime Minister, the President and the Foreign Minister not to be examined for courtesy. We had been thinking to import some machineries which even the Government's Codes for import or "Franco Valuta" did not allow. Hence, you join in and facilitate our work by advising the airport customs office that the machineries we would be illegally smuggling in as if they belonged to the PM or any senior rank minister's guests and you would earn your own share after we sold the items." Very deceiving and honey coated – wasn't it?

> *"Dishonest money dwindles away, but whoever gathers money little by little makes it grow."* (Proverbs 13:11) Wealth gotten by vanity shall be diminished but he that gathered by labour shall increase.

I told him, "You are totally out of your mind. You are insane! How dare you ask me to be part of this kind of scam. No, thank you, for your disgusting offer – I will pay for my Pepsi." It even surprises me to date how some people's minds are wired this way. Why are people not satisfied with what they earn with their labour? These were the kind of people killing my beloved country, Ethiopia. They should have known whatever illegal and selfish things they were doing was paramount to killing the country's economy or painfully writing on the skins of our poor people who had never seen a decent life except for the few.

His thoughts were exactly what a headless chicken would think of me in light of getting involved with crazy criminal activities. Even worse! A few people like this one here and there could hamper our country's economic growth and development because of their corruption and illegal deeds. They needed to be stamped out by all means! I heard in the news in regards to Ethiopia that corruption is rampant even in the present days. It is very miserable!

After graduation, I did not get a job right away and did not earn money for my living. During this period, I had three major incidents of people begging me to give them some money. I was not able to support them by giving money and I felt hurt.

The first incident was that I bumped into a young man around Ghion hotel. He had on white trainers with black stripes and was dressed far better than me at that time. He asked me for some money to top it up for him so that he could buy a medicine for his child. The second was around Kazanchis, a name of a place in Addis Ababa where a woman who carried her baby on her back asked me for money. The last one was in a place called Gergi where a young boy asked me for some money so that he could buy bread to eat. In all these three cases I was in tears and asked God why He was doing this to me. In all the above three cases I did not have money to provide for them. I felt miserably sad that I was not able to give.

On the other hand, once I was employed financial windfalls started to shower on me. I was blessed to bless others. There were so many people who gave me gifts in kind and financially at different times for I had been their accompaniment. I realised in life that for some people giving is a painful experience and for some others it is a joy. Besides, please allow me to expose the myth of giving in secret a bit in detail here. Now I know that I am treading on dangerous ground. I do not believe that when we choose to give, we broadcast it on BBC or CNN and shout it out to the world to win the approval of people. On the contrary, I believe with all my heart that the motive behind your giving is a vital link to receiving your harvest. If you give for self-gratification or pride, I do not believe you will receive the abundance that would come to you as when you give out of a pure heart. **Very recently in the early morning of Sunday 22ⁿᵈ October 2023 in Nashville, Tennessee, Mekdes Girma Sahlu gave me a very special gift to be delivered to my daughter Abigail and uttered, "Merid 'nebis eko neh'" meaning "Merid, you are the best!" That was an incredible lesson to me – to give a gift to someone and admire the receiver. Mekdes is in a new level of humbleness and kindness – a little kindness goes a long way. May God bless you and your family for eternity!**

> *"In everything I did, I showed you that by this kind of hard work we must help the weak, remembering the words the Lord Jesus himself said: 'It is more blessed to give than to receive.'"* (Acts 20:35)

Brigadier General Dr Emmanuel Ndahiro, Rwanda's former Chief of Intelligence and Security who was also a physician, security adviser and spokesman to President Paul Kagame, was once transiting via Addis Ababa. I was advised to meet and take care of him in the VIP Lounge by the Chief of Cabinet in the Foreign Minister's Office.

I met him by the steps of the plane and took him to the VIP Lounge and served him with fresh orange juice. At the time I really did not have any details of the gentleman as Mr Yemane Kidane, the Chief of the Cabinet in the Foreign Minister's Office, simply said please meet and look after my friend.

As we were chatting, Dr Emmanuel told me that he was an

advisor to President Paul Kagame. He did not say more – he was a man of few words! He did not boast and he acted like a very ordinary person despite being a very influential person in his country – Rwanda. He told me that once somebody came to his home and gave him a very expensive gift saying, "Thank you for saving my life in the hospital with your life-saving surgery." He added, "I did not even know the gentleman as he could be any one of my patients. I operated on several of them."

He presented me with an envelope and said, "You are a wonderful person treating me in a very respectful way whilst I was waiting for my connecting flight." I protested not to take the envelope and said to him that I was just doing my job. I did not expect to have any reward for doing my job. He wished me all the best in my future career and he insisted that I take his gift – seven hundred US Dollars – probably ten months of my salary in less than an hour for a friendly chat with a senior politician of Rwanda. This could not be anything less than God's grace and favour.

Our Egypt Ambassador back then, Ms Konjit Sinegiorgis, called me on my mobile from Cairo to look after a Commissioner from Bangladesh who was transiting via Ethiopia to Ouagadougou, Burkina Faso. I did look after him in the Ministerial VIP Lounge. Bangladesh people are always friendly and close to me both in London and Surrey. What lovely people! He told me that I had something special in me and wanted to leave something special of his own so that we could remember each other. He was an older gentleman who had his own family. I remember him still today, but does he? What was that something special in me which even a Muslim gentleman witnessed? Holy Spirit – the Spirit of the Living God which dwells in my heart. Praise the Lord! *"Don't you know that you yourselves are God's temple and that God's Spirit dwells in your midst?" (1 Corinthians 3:16)* He took off his new neck-tie and

said, "I would leave my most beautiful and new cravat with you
– enjoy wearing it!" To this date I always wear this neck-tie with
beautiful yellow flowers on it. I have had more than sixty neck-ties
all my life but none of them match this one.

Every time I wore it people, women and men alike, would tell
me that it was the most beautiful neck-tie that they ever saw on me.
What a kind gift from someone with whom I had been about thirty
minutes. This is how the love of God operates among people who
fear Him. May God bless me with the fear of the Lord! May He also
blesses you too! (Proverbs 9:10) *"The fear of the Lord is the beginning
of wisdom: and the knowledge of the Holy One is understanding."*
(Proverbs 10:27) *"The fear of the LORD adds length to life, but the
years of the wicked are cut short."*

The Hungarian ambassador resident in Nairobi and accredited
to Ethiopia was the most touching story I have for you to read.
Keep on reading and see for yourselves that a day fixed on your life's
journey might not change from happening. Do you believe that
our lives are destined to a prearranged programme by the Master
King of kings? In the same token, predestination in Christianity
means the doctrine that God has eternally chosen those whom he
intends to save. What are your thoughts on this?

His programmes changed three times to tally his coming from
Nairobi, Kenya to Ethiopia with the late President Negasso Gidada's
schedule to present his letter of credentials as full ambassador
extraordinary and plenipotentiary. His name was Antal Annus, the
Hungarian ambassador to Kenya. I was the one who was assigned
to take him to the Foreign Minister to present a copy of his letter
of credence and the original one to the President.

In the morning I called the Hilton Hotel from my office in
the headquarters and asked him what time I should send him an
official palace car. He said, "Please do not send me one. I would

appreciate if you could come over and walk down with me to the Foreign Ministry at first and then to the President Office." I agreed with him as he had a better plan for a change. I went to the Hilton Hotel ten minutes earlier than the appointment time. I am always on time for my appointments – be it personal or work related. He came to the guest area of the hotel and off we went to the Ministry.

He was dressed so elegantly and had his hat on his head. He was a former minister in his country before he was assigned as an ambassador. What was more, he had a family in Nairobi, Kenya – a wife and a daughter. We went to the Minister's office and he presented his copy. Next, we walked down to the National Palace where the President resides. I briefed him with the simple national protocol procedure as the following.

Step One – When you are about three steps away from the President, you pause next to me, facing him.

Step Two – I will announce you to the President with a loud voice saying, "Your Excellency, Mr President – the ambassador of the Republic of Hungary is here to present his original letter of credence as an Ambassador Extraordinary and Plenipotentiary."

Step Three – As soon as I have finished announcing, you move one step forward and introduce yourself to the President.

Step Four – The President will extend his hand to shake yours. You shake his hand and after brief welcoming conversations he will invite you to sit on his right hand side and then there's time for a bilateral discussion of your country with ours.

The General Director of Europe and America and other relevant people will be there during the discussion. Once you have finished your discussion and taken ceremonial photos with the President, you will find me in the entrance guest room – we could meet there and take you back to your hotel.

After the ceremony and the bilateral talks were finished, we met up in the place where we had agreed. We went back to the Hilton Hotel and he invited me for dinner in the evening to celebrate the occasion. We sat together in the dining room, enjoying our meals and talking about certain matters in our respective countries. Moreover, we talked about some personal and family issues. Suddenly, the Brazilian Ambassador resident in Kenya came to our table and asked him if he could postpone his flight and travel with him to see the historical routes of Ethiopia. Ethiopia's historical routes like Lalibela, Axum, Gondar and Bahir Dar, Lake Tana Monasteries and more. Discover Ethiopia's cultural routes too, including South Omo Valley tribes and experience how magnificent this country is!

The two of them knew each other in Nairobi but the Hungarian Ambassador declined the invitation saying, "Tomorrow morning my wife and my daughter will be waiting for me at Jomo Kenyatta International Airport. I cannot cancel my flight!" Could he not? At the end of our dinner, he gave me two bottles of Budweiser whiskies as a takeaway gift. It was a generous gift from the Hungarian Ambassador – almost certainly the last gift he made before his last breath.

Next day, on November 26, 1996, he was travelling enroute from Addis Ababa to Nairobi on a Boeing 767-200ER, flight number IATA – ET961. The flight was hijacked by three Ethiopians who were seeking asylum in Australia. The plane crash-landed in the Indian Ocean near Grande Comore, Comoros Islands due to fuel exhaustion and 125 of the 175 passengers and crew on board, including the three hijackers, died.

The Hungarian Ambassador was among those who died and I was in tears for weeks and probably months. I could not forget the simplicity and kindness he had shown me. He was a gentleman with amazing attributes. RIP Ambassador Antal Annus of Hungary. May your family have gotten the comfort they needed from God

Almighty. **Kindness is a gift everyone can afford. How can I be
kind to you today? Kindness is our language, let us talk.**
Email me – mergicho@gmail.com

*"Who comforts us in all our troubles, so that we can comfort those
in any trouble with the comfort we ourselves receive from God."*
(2 Corinthians 1:4)

More gifts in kind from our ambassadors – Ambassador Konjit
blessed me with three pairs of shoes and I still wear one of them after
twenty-five years. They are shiny brown, a beautiful pair of shoes.
President H.E. Ms Sahle-Work Zewde, our former Ambassador in
several countries before taking the new post, always buys me a liquor
gift called "Teachers" whisky brand predicting I would be a teacher
in my future life. Most Ethiopian ambassadors either bring me
chocolates, neck-ties, shirts and some African costumes. May God
bless those who are alive. I knew some of them have gone – RIP.

I received several hundreds of red level and black level whiskies
from the Diplomatic Missions in Addis Ababa every Christmas
and New Year seasons. That was the tradition of Embassies to say,
"Thank you for our mutual understanding, partnerships and joint
efforts to work together throughout the year!" and renew their
bilateral relationships with the host country's officials.

Possibly, I was receiving the most gifts next to the Foreign
Minister, H.E. Mr Seyoum Mesfin from the entire Ministry.
There was no need for me either to be corrupted or steal from
the government who put their trust in me. I was receiving gifts
from people who were happy with the way I treated them with my
pleasant personality. I was enjoying my life at its best and living
my dream of giving – a very simple and joyful life! However, it
is good to take note that I wouldn't be stealing even if I did not

receive a penny or gifts in kind from other people. My early lesson was a stepping stone in turning my life 180-degrees.

Apart from these I used to welcome dignitaries, senior government ministers, special envoys, investors, prime ministers and presidents of other countries all by myself when they were visiting Ethiopia on an unofficial visit. I would not be sitting in their counterparts' seats in the premier and ministerial lounges but would sit next to them and facilitate the things I should, like telephone calling with my senior government officials of the time and serving them with the best refreshments of fresh juices and hot meals from the Ethiopian Restaurant in honour of my government and country. I was very careful with the codes of diplomacy and foreign policy!

For instance, to mention a few of the dignitaries, I met President H.E. Mr Esayas Afeworki of Eritrea and President H.E. Mr Kabila of Democratic Republic of Congo one time each, and President H.E. Mr Paul Kagame of Rwanda three times all by myself when he was coming on an unofficial basis to Ethiopia. Especially H.E. Mr Paul Kagame, I accompanied and drove him in my Landcruiser to the Prime Minister's Office as he did not want an official palace car. Several ex-presidents and ex-prime ministers of other governments were welcomed by myself on many occasions including the former president of the USA – H.E. Mr Jimmy Carter.

The following three incidents still make me laugh and wonder when I remember them.

Once we were welcoming a high-level delegation led by President H.E. Mr Esayas. It was a honeymoon time for the two governments, namely Ethiopia and Eritrea. We had no information that the First Lady of Eritrea would be accompanying the President and hence our preparation focused only on the president to give him a bouquet of flowers. Then, we were notified at short notice that she was in the plane ready to disembark. Thus, I took the bouquet of flowers from the flower girl and split it into two – one for the president and the other for his wife, making my government and country proud with God-given insights, courage and wisdom.

At another time I was welcoming the First Lady of Uganda with her Ambassador, Ambassador H.E. Mr Butajira who was resident in Addis Ababa. I guess someone had informed her that the deputy foreign minister would be welcoming her at the airport. I did not know the details of what she had been informed by our Embassy in Kampala, Uganda or her own Ministry of Foreign Affairs. But I welcomed her at the steps of the plane and she was addressing me as "Your Excellency, Dr Tekeda Alemu" which wasn't me!

It is possible to infer that there could have been an original plan of welcoming the First Lady by a higher official, which I did not know about. Had I known that I could have contacted the Tower personnel/Flight Control to inform her that the deputy was not at the airport to welcome her. Information is power! Anyway, I had a chance to inform her that I was not the person whom she was expecting to address and told her who I was at the most appropriate time. I also tipped the Ambassador that I was from a small town called Butajira, akin his name. With my pieces of advice, he went to visit Butajira before his tour of work ended.

The third one was when the US Transport Minister was coming with his charter flight and thirteen delegate members without an entry visa to Ethiopia. His chartered flight was landing four in the morning in Ethiopian local time. Under those circumstances, I needed to stay all the evening and night in the airport office. It was sad that there was no bed facility in the airport office at the time.

However, when I was one of the members of the Facilitation Committee of the new terminal in the airport, I recommended that the Foreign Office at the airport should have a bedroom facility. I hope the current officers working at the airport office are enjoying the fruits of what their predecessors proposed for their care and comfort when they did not have one for themselves – thinking and doing something good ahead of time for the next generation. Dream – Plan – Do!

The late H.E. Dr Abdulmegid Hussein, the then Transport and Communication Minister on the Ethiopian side, became relieved the moment he saw me in the VIP Lounge early in the morning. He was sitting with the American Ambassador H.E. Mr David Shinn and other Embassy staff at the time. Mr Hiruy Ammanuel, the General Director of Europe and America was also there. The moment he saw me entering the VIP Lounge, H.E. Dr Abdulmegid stood up from where he was sat on the sofa to greet me. All who were seated with him stood up all together, to whom the Minister was respecting. He loudly announced, "This is the gentleman whom we were looking for and who could solve our guests' problems who are coming without entry visas."

Indeed, I was the one who could advise the airport immigration office about entry visas. I felt ten feet high for the warm welcome and unexpected introduction I had received by the Minister and all who were with him. Ambassador David Shin arranged a luncheon in the American Embassy in honour of me not long ago from this occasion. Professor Sir Myles Wickstead, Ambassador of the United Kingdom at that time organised luncheons in my honour twice before I was sent as a diplomat to his country. On those three working luncheons I expertly and diplomatically sold the image of my country to the level this great country of ours deserves. They were resident ambassadors in our country and had their own diplomatic sources, but there were some intricate things which a citizen deeply understands more than foreign diplomats.

I advised the airport immigration office beforehand for a speedy service of entry visas for the American delegation led by the transport minister. As a representative of the Foreign Office, everything must have been channelled through me. Respecting the rule of law agreed between the Ministry and Immigration and Security Authority was of paramount importance to the smooth functioning of government affairs.

H.E. Dr Abdulmegid welcomed the thirteen delegates led by the USA transport minister along with Ambassador Shinn to Ethiopia and we let them enjoy their stay. Will the Americans reciprocate if this kind of scenario happens on their side? As a matter of quid pro quo in diplomacy, it should be mutually beneficial to both countries. In the secular life, whatever I am doing for you today, I will anticipate you will do the same when a similar scenario happens on the other side. The Scriptural verse in support of this kind of good deed is "*Do to others as you would have them do to you*". (Luke 6:31)

H.E. Dr Abdulmegid was a very humble person who passed away whilst he was serving for our country as an ambassador in the United Nations Permanent Missions. I used to hear from our Cabinet Ministers that the late Prime Minister H.E. Mr Meles Zenawi used to call him a "Misguided Missile!" as he was an honest and straightforward minister. He used to speak his mind with no fear of his ideas being accepted or not. He was a brave gentleman. Do we have now cabinet members who could necessarily challenge and air out their fruitful views to the present Prime Minister H.E. Dr Abiy Ahmed? We genuinely need people like that who bring fresh ideas for leadership consumption.

There was no such thing as a visa on arrival at that time. Those are the incidents which led to a provision of a visa on arrival afterwards. Solution-oriented people proposed visas to be available on arrival from both the Foreign Ministry as well as the Immigration and Security Authority of Ethiopia. Everything has its own significant steps and long journeys over time to see a smooth operational process in immigration acts and laws. Nothing was ready-made and came down from Heaven like manna. We had think-tank groups across different ministries to do researches on certain policies which could benefit our country as well as those willing to work in partnerships.

A think-tank is an organisation that gathers a group of inter-disciplinary scholars to perform research around particular policies, issues or ideas. Topics addressed in think-tanks can cover a wide range, including social policy, public policy, economic policy, political strategy, culture and technology. Problem-solving attitudes of members of staff in the Immigration and Security Authority along with my colleagues in the Ministry of Foreign Affairs was commendable to this task – we were all together in this.

In other instances, if there were any aeroplanes coming towards our airspace, I was the one who would be consulted after midnight to give the go-ahead or deny the plane from landing. Only if I was in a dilemma with any sound decision making should I call and wake up the Chief of the National Protocol from his sleep. I would check for what purpose the plane was coming to Ethiopia without having the necessary flight permission ahead of time, who and what was on board. I had the uncompromised passion and conscience of dealing with matters meticulously to the highest standard in light of my country's national interest. Who would not do that for a responsibility like this?

This drama of seeing off and welcoming of the late Prime Minister H.E. Meles Zenawi was always getting my full attention. For your information, Meles was a shrewd politician but also a man who could trust others around him. For instance, I could get him a caffe macchiato from *Sky Restaurant* by one of my trusted waiters, Gash Kore, and he used to drink it straight away without any doubt. I knew most presidents and prime ministers send their closest security personnel to scrutinise the preparation of whatever drinks or meals they ordered. Look out, there was no security to accompany me when I was serving him his hot drink from the Ethiopian Restaurant.

We used to call and advise the cabinet ministers to come and do the ceremony of the arrival and departure of the premiership. On the top of that I supervised and monitored civil aviation protocol department for the red-carpet ceremony. I needed to observe the arrival and departure protocol setting as they were different. I would line up our ministers according to their seniority and observe how they would react when the Prime Minister either comes to his plane or gets out of it. Some of the ministers would not allow even a wind to come and move away their neck-ties from their chests if that was possible. There was that absolute respect and dignity from all the ministers to the Prime Minister. Proverbs 24:21 states, *"Fear the Lord and the king, my son, and do not join with rebellious officials."*

We would tip one minister to walk along with the premier depending on the nature of his foreign visit. For instance, if the visit abroad had got something to do with agriculture, we would advise the agriculture minister to walk along and brief the premier about agricultural issues which the premier needed to give priority to in dealing with the bilateral diplomacy with the host country of the foreign visit. That was the tradition as far as the Ethiopian National Protocol was concerned during that time.

In my heart I always think of Jesus – the King of Kings, Lord of Lords who died for the sins of every single human being on earth. Why did we find it difficult to give our full attention to Him when He deserves the most? He reconciled us with God, the Father so that we could enjoy everlasting life in heaven with Him.

"You are worthy. Our Lord and God, to receive glory and honour and power for you created all things, by your will they were created and have their being." (Revelations 4:11)

CHAPTER 3

Zebidar is love

"If I have the gift of prophecy and can fathom all mysteries and all knowledge, and if I have a faith that can move mountains, but do not have love, I am nothing." (1 Corinthians 13:2).

Anyone who has climbed up these Chains of Mountains of Love will be full of happiness and bright hopes for their future life. Moreover, they will also know that it raises their spirits and makes them feel spectacular sensations. The God of Zebidar Who created it marvellously and beautifully is LOVE.

I am glad I have done it once by myself and would love to do it again with a group of tourists who will be interested to travel – please email me on mergicho@gmail.com if you are interested. Besides, my mum showed me three stars…

"He determines the number of stars and calls them by name." (Psalm 147:3)

I am looking forward to climb up the Love Mountains of Zebidar once more in the very near future with whoever wants to go with me. Probably a group of British tourists who are eager to visit this amazing country – ETHIOPIA – thirteen months of sunshine.

Giving love to Friends of Ethiopia.

Ethiopia is a country split diagonally by an act of nature – the cleavage known as the Great Rift Valley which stretches from the Dead Sea between Israel and Jordan and down the length of East Africa to enter the sea at Mozambique. It enters Ethiopia from the Red Sea through Eritrea in a 'Y' formation north of the border with Djibouti, then runs southward, producing a chain of small lakes beyond Addis Ababa, to leave the country at Lake Turkana (formerly Rudolf) and enter Kenya. (1)

William Paley used a watch – a timepiece to rationally and theologically argue the existence of God. He was born in July 1743 and died on May 29, 1805 at age 65. He was an English clergyman, a Christian apologist, a philosopher, and a utilitarian. He is best known for his natural theology and his argument for the existence of God, rather than several gods. The argument follows that if it was designed like this, then someone or something must have designed it.

Paley's Design Argument is that the universe exhibits design through its implied purpose and through regularity. The main argument being from purpose explains why Paley's argument is also called the 'Teleological Argument', telos being the Greek for 'end', or 'purpose'. The watch is a complicated thing, and it has a designer. Paley compares the watch with the world, and the world is even more complex. Thus, it also must have a designer, and he said the only person capable of designing the world had to be God, therefore God exists.

"The heavens declare the glory of God; the skies proclaim the work of his hands" (Psalm 19:1).

Life is beautiful in Ethiopia, no matter how difficult it could be for some time – things will change. Hope. There is a brighter life ahead and Ethiopia's future hope of greatness, prosperity, stability and peace is inevitable. I am grateful to my Creator every moment of every day for His Divine Protection, Deep Caring and that I am originally from Ethiopia. Love the life you live, and you will live the life you love. Love without regret and with a thanksgiving heart. Life is a gift – live it merrily and showing love and kindness to others. Good relationships with family and friends are one of God's greatest gifts. Treasure them, thank God for them and keep them close – so your friendship will last a lifetime. I thank God for He gave me families and friends all my life.

Zebidar's perspective of love is an exceptional and outstanding one! It appreciates all God's creations – the trees, the bushes and even the thorns which grow on it. It has never grown tired of them, rather it is deeply grateful that they gave beauty to it. Zebidar also treasures the grasses and the flowers which cover it and more importantly the people who live in the surrounding areas and beyond. The Ethiopian people are incredible resources for the economic development of the country and safeguarding of its territorial sovereignty.

Zebidar argues people enjoy the sunrise, sunshine and sunset. They also enjoy the plants, flowers, the beaches of the seas and the oceans. Moreover, they are thrilled with the crescent and full moons. However, they don't look appreciatively at another human being who is created in the image and likeness of God. Why do some people not cherish meeting other human beings to the level expected? The human community ought to dig deep to know the root causes for this and take some corrective measures before it is too late.

The Love Mountains are puzzled with this attitude of humankind for centuries. But the Creator appreciates His creations and they are important to him more than any other things in the universe. That was why He sent His only Son to save the people. *"For God so loved the world that he gave his one and only Son, that whoever believes in him shall not perish but have eternal life."* (John 3:16)

All that God created is beyond the human's full comprehension. Every person in the world is entirely unique, down to their fingerprint, the colour of the iris in your eyes is unique to every single individual and nobody else in the world has the exact same coloured eye like yours as well as your DNA. We need to respond to God's greatness by praising Him for all He has created. God is good all the time!

On the other hand, the colourful traditional celebration of epiphany – the Ethiopian Timket holiday – is an outstanding one. Especially the epiphany celebration in Gondar, where my wife comes from, is phenomenal! By the same token, Butajira's epiphany celebration far exceeds expectations and is peculiar. I guess all the different regions have their own variations and uniqueness.

On the last day of this ritual and spiritual holiday, the young men and young women from all the surrounding small villages of Butajira will come to St Mary Church accompanying the Ark of St Mary. They sang, danced and praised God during the celebration. After dancing and singing, the young men who were ready for marriage would hold their lemons in their hands and try to put them in the hands of the young ladies with whom they had found love.

By any chance if the young men succeeded in putting the lemons into their respective young women's palms, voluntarily or by force, then that would be considered as their proposal had been accepted. Otherwise, the young women needed to fight with all their might and strength not to open up their palms for the lemons if they did not approve of the potential husband. I call it – The Lemon Therapy of the Beginning of Romantic Love.

Once when we were in our Secondary School, I travelled with my friends a few kilometres to witness another traditional and cultural ceremony in a place called Ticho. This one had a different social fabric, flavour and texture. The main actors were called, "Muyetes" and would be carrying live snakes on their shoulders and fed the snakes butter in a bowl. No one was allowed to see them straight into their eyes when they were dancing and chanting, making a circle. You have to bow down probably to show respect to them and agree that they are more powerful than the onlookers. If someone did not bow down, they would be whipped. However, after the event a similar lemon therapy was taking place like the epiphany religious holidays.

Having said that, let me cast a light upon my social communication skills. Social communication refers to the use of verbal (spoken language) and nonverbal (eye gaze, facial expression, gestures) communication in social situations, to tell other people what you want, express feelings, relate to other people and develop meaningful relationships.

The first time I had a brief normal conversation with a girl was when I was in Grade 10. Before this incident happened in a jail randomly, I never remember having one except a few words with my neighbour who happened to share a common fence between our properties while exchanging our notebooks. This conversation never went further on either the girl asking me to give her my book and vice versa. Our exchange of words was very limited. "Science book?" and my answer was so short – "Okay". And handing books over the fence. You could see for yourselves that was not really a great social communication, at least on my side. However, when we were both in higher educations, we started to communicate a great deal and performed better. Hello Selamawit Gebremichael, wherever you are, may God's richest blessings be upon you today and forever. Even more, may those blessings flow through you to touch the lives of everyone you meet in your life's journey.

When I was in Grade 10, there was this notion that academically bright students should also participate in some activities of the Ethiopian Socialist Revolution celebration. Besides, we were instructed to study the principles of socialism and communism in our local administration centre commonly known as the "kebele". As a result, my name was passed to the local administration from my school and I became part of it. I started to train marching like the army for a military show on the 12th of September – famously called Meskerem 2 – Revolution Day.

Whilst on training, the militia man who was in charge commanded the marching youth to turn around. I did not hear him giving the command so I kept on marching by myself as I was the first person in the row while the entire group turned around. I did not see them and kept on marching by myself. It was not funny!

Nevertheless, the militia man shouted at me, pointing out his finger on my head that I was anti-revolutionary. Humiliating. Furthermore, he screamed that I could be a protestant Christian believer and I needed to be sent to prison. This was an absolute abuse of power – the great political thinkers say, "Absolute power corrupts absolutely". There was religious persecution in Ethiopia during that time. There was no freedom of practising your faith the way you wanted and people were being jailed for several years as a result.

He called his assistant and I was sent to jail. I had never been imprisoned before and tried to imagine what it would look like on my way. He threw me in the jail and after a while a young girl came to see one of the prisoners there. She brought soup for him and she offered me some saying, "May you please try this? My mum is the one who prepared it." She was a generous Muslim girl.

Even in prison God sent me someone to look after me. She shone like a beautiful beam of light in my heart. God's FAVOUR! She was kind, indeed very kind to offer something to eat to someone whom even she did not know, I was touched by her pure kindness as a young boy who had never experienced something like that before.

The prisoner whom she was looking after had been working in partnership with her mother – they smuggle coffee from a place called Hossana to other places for trading. I carried her beauty and kindness in my heart for a very long time. I found joy and peace in my brief conversation with her. To your surprise, the prisoner and that very young girl married and created their own family. May God continue to bless them for eternity!

I was released from the prison in the evening but I should not have been sent without good reason. Read the Declaration of Human Rights – 1948. My human right was infringed in daylight even if my experience in the prison was not that bad at all. Albeit, I do not want to go to prison unless I ought to visit prisoners to comfort them, give them hope that there will be a beautiful life beyond the bar when they are released and also this small experience of being imprisoned encouraged me to involve myself in prison education in the UK. Once, I was teaching in Wandsworth prison for a brief time.

I received a call on Wednesday the 8th of November 2023 from my childhood friend Nigussie Kassahun Desta, Denver, Colorado. We enjoyed talking about our lively and lovely childhood memories. In about less than a quarter of an hour we were able to visit our small town Butajira and every village inside it. The power of our thinking was so immense in that we travelled thousands of miles together in seconds and he told me this – that I wrote him a strong romantic letter in which I described his childhood love as ". . . you are the Cinderella of my life . . ." I was flabbergasted! He had an awesome long memory. Thank you and may the Lord bless you and your family for eternity!

In fact, I vividly remember my first would-be-love letter I wrote to a girl in my classroom when I was in Grade 5. I am not sure whether it was before or after my stealing experience of the farm. Did it matter?

The letter read something like this –

Dear _____,
You saw me under the big tree.
I saw you too.
Why?
Sincerely yours,
Merid.

I still remember her name. I just did not want to write it down in this book. That was a very reflective love letter for a Grade 5 student.

Wasn't it a very romantic letter trying to find out why she was looking at me under the shadow of the big tree? She did not reply in writing or verbally on account of her reasons to look at me under the shade of the big tree. If she did, I would have remembered it. What was I going to do if she was in love with me? Could a ten- or eleven-year-old be romantically attracted to the opposite sex? But what is love?

Romantic love is often very emotional. Two people are attracted to each other, and strong feelings develop between them. This is often what people mean when they say they are in love – they have strong romantic feelings toward another person. There is nothing wrong with this, of course – there is definitely an emotional side to true love.

But the problem with merely romantic love is that it gradually fades as time goes on. Unfortunately, when this happens a couple may decide that there is no longer any hope for love in their relationship and decide to end the marriage.

True love includes romantic love, but it is more than that. True love involves a commitment to each other and settled determination to be kind and considerate to the other person instead of selfish.

Love, you see, is more than a feeling – it is also an action. (2)

This world is full of lust for power, money, success and sex. I would like to write a few words about the lust for sex from someone whom I encountered in my early years of work during my time in the Foreign Ministry. This incident happened when I was working as a Third Secretary in the Ministry of Foreign Affairs of Ethiopia. My boss ordered me to go to the airport, to meet and greet a lady who was coming from Washington DC, USA for a conference called the Global Coalition Conference for Africa. It was an international conference whereby delegates from all over Africa attended. The World Bank former President Mr Robert S McNamara was also part of this international conference.

I met this tall, young lady at the steps of the plane, served her via the VIP Lounge and took her to the Hilton Hotel where she was staying until she finished the conference. The next day, she asked me to go to the airport with her and meet one of her colleagues. We went and welcomed another young lady, who was a mixed race of white American with Central Africa. She was gorgeous. The latter asked me to take her to a nightclub and we went to Shames night club – that was the first time I ever went to a nightclub. The scene was horrible and neither of us liked it – as a result, we left the nightclub early.

I was working for the national interests of my country at an elementary level – making a good impression on workers of the World Bank so that the institution would be happy to give us a loan. These were the kind of things which brings about good gestures from the global financial institutions like the World Bank (WB) and the International Monetary Fund (IMF). In diplomacy, every single step act of goodness counts. The means justifies the end result! Do everything possible which is good without limitations under the sun. Don't be controversial! Contribute your small effort and make a difference – every little helps!! Even the smallest things are helpful towards a goal *that add up to a big difference.*

However, later in life I learned that the big beasts (governments) could misbehave behind the screen against their own nationals who are living abroad by agreeing to unfair deportation with some countries for the sake of financial gain or securing a loan from the World Bank or International Monetary Fund.

A day before departure date of the delegates who participated in the conference, the Ethiopian Finance minister was holding a dinner banquet in honour of the African Finance Ministers and the World Bank. Thus, the World Bank lady whom I met first and

I were due to have a discussion as to the seating arrangements for the dinner table. We agreed to meet in the Lounge of the Hilton Hotel. I went in the morning and notified her of my arrival through the phone. She invited me to come to her bedroom and I went to her.

As it was a rainy day, I had this big "green, yellow and red" multicoloured umbrella to protect me from the rain. A big beautiful smile appeared on her face and she said, "You know, Mr Merid, I need a big umbrella like yours to cover . . ." She opened her gown and exposed her private parts to me – that was a sexual assault! There is this famous quote which says, "Never trust a beautiful woman especially one who is interested in you."

Her lust to have sex with me was crystal clear. Lust is a feeling of having a strong sexual desire for another person. She was crazy – she showed me her private parts and sat down on the edge of the bed, her eyes gazing at me. My brain was racing, trying to find a way out, not to make a wrong turn and get carried away by the whole drama of "Come over and get inside of me". Like always I prayed my short instant prayer in my heart, "God save me!" Then, I needed to run away from her bedroom lest I would fall in her trap. Thus, I mumbled, "Please meet me in the 'Guest Area'," and ran away. I am glad that God helped me not to commit that particular sin! This is God's Divine Protection and I would not be able to do it by myself.

Like God had saved me from the car accident a few years before this incident (reflected on in Chapter 11) He saved me from a potential international sex crime. *"Before they call, I will answer while they are still speaking, I will hear."* (Isaiah 65:24)

Was it a pure lust for sex or a trap to make a sensational sex crime news? At the time the Clinton–Lewinsky sex scandal was very hot news. Their sexual relationship lasted between 1995 and

1997. Monica Lewinsky was a 22-year-old White House intern whereas Bill Clinton was the 42nd President of the USA.

On a different note, after we saw off the Foreign Minister abroad, his driver and nephew, Mr Teklekiros Teferi, offered me a ride in his car if I needed to go somewhere. I thought of surprising my younger sister, Hiywot, who was studying Economics at the Faculty of Business and Economics, Addis Ababa University, at the time. So I asked him to drive me to Addis Ababa University. We went off from the airport, drove on Bole Road via Meskel Square, crossing the road between the Foreign Office and the Hilton Hotel, through Arat Kilo and arrived at the university. We found out my sister was busy with her friends going to Menelik hospital to visit one of their friends who had been in the hospital bed at the time.

My university life was chaotic. I had been through a wave of sight loves. The most pertinent one was about the young girl whom I saw on my first day in the university. I was going inside the compound and she was leaving by the main entrance gate of the Social Sciences College, Sidist Kilo University. I turned around and stared at her for a long time until she disappeared from my sight, and I muttered, "Heaven Sent!"

After she left the compound, I went to the lecture hall in the New Class Rooms (NCR) where Freshman students were registering. In my heart, I hoped to see her again. A promising challenge or chance was born inside me on my first day in university. Or was it a pure threat, or could I use it as a stepping stone at least in my future relationships?

I recall I developed some kind of sensing her in my surrounding areas. If I felt she was around, 100% of the time I was right: she would be there. She was tall, dark-chocolate skin and her wide, round face was framed by a mass of curly black hair, her eyes were kind and like sparkling velvet-brown diamonds and always seemed to dance with laughter. How was it possible that I was attracted to her?

Soon enough I discovered that she was a second-year student. Sight-love knows no seniority. Next, other students discovered that I was a victim of love. Looking at her made me sweat – like cold ice at the back of my body. Sometimes, I was struck dead with terror when I accidentally came face-to-face with her. At other times, my heart was beating painfully fast and banging against my ribs. What am I going to do? Should I use her friend (the one studying Law) as an instrument to reach her after I discovered her friend's uncle was my childhood friend (Mr Belete Demisew Wudmatas)? "No, I should not do that!" I argued to myself.

I told my mum about my love story at the end of year one when I went home for summer holidays. She listened to me without interrupting and giving any positive or negative comment on the subject. I knew what she was doing – she was praying silently and fervently whether giving my heart to this young lady was the right thing to do or not. She had a lot on her plate to pray for and I am eternally grateful to her for her spiritual devotions.

No one who has ever lived on this planet could give a sound judgement and timely advice for anyone in the community like my mum. My mum had been through the trials of life – she had walked in a steeper and longer road of life. As a result, she had a great personality of not judging people but praying enthusiastically and uninterruptedly, that they would have a better life.

The sight-love I contracted was causing lots of problems in my academic life. I needed to talk to the young lady with whom I had sight-love – accept her verdict of having me as her boyfriend or not. Either way, I ought to have a talk with her. I studied her Exam schedules by going to her department's notice board and decided to talk to her when she was coming out of the exam hall with the piece of advice and encouragement I got from a friend – Mr Ayenew

Bitewlign. By then, she was a third year Management student and I was a sophomore.

I had been waiting for her by the exam hall ready to talk to her but lost my courage of a face-to-face encounter. Where did my courage of Grade 5 go? Looking back, I could see my advisor lacked wisdom. How could someone declare that they were in love with another right after a semester exam? She might have been disappointed with her exam and could have slapped me on the face. Thank God, I did not ask her after her exams – it was not good timing!

However, the wave of thinking about her was intensifying during my exam times and I was not studying effectively. Can somebody say "No!" to love, I wondered. I could not! There are two schools of thoughts in philosophy about love. One school says, "You cannot say 'no' to love. It is something natural and goes beyond one's ability to reject it as it happens." This school of thought supports my reality of life.

The other school of thought suggests that anybody could say 'no' to love especially when she/he had a moral obligation to accomplish. For instance, in my case, I joined university to pursue further education and not to fall in love with someone. In the eyes of the school of thought which affirms I could reject the sight-love I was experiencing – I was a failure. I did not fulfil my duty of studying hard to be successful in my academics. Nonetheless, it was not that easy to reject it either. That I did not manage to talk to her was a total disaster whereas that I continued to love her was human's nature. But, all this time, did she know that I had ever loved her? I really do not think so.

My third year was a tragedy. I scored "F" in International Law as I was not able to study at all. Moreover, the worst scenario was when I scored zero out of forty for my local administration course.

In sharp contrast to this, I benefited in my coursework as I scored the highest in my batch – fifty-seven out of sixty. This was the time my effort was praised by an English professor Dr Mekonnen Disasa (Chapter One). Furthermore, I was offered a retake of my International Law course in the form of course work and I scored "A". Nonetheless, a result "A" in resit is considered as a "B" so that it was recorded as a "B" grade in my student copy.

Once in Kennedy Library, a student one year senior than me had a group picture in which the young lady with whom I had a crush was included. He gave me the pictures to see them. Instantly the guy found out that I liked that particular young lady without me telling him. There were other girls in the group pictures as well. How he realised that I had fallen for her was beyond my understanding to this date. His name was Girum meaning "Wonder". Did he have the ability to read through people's minds? I wondered.

I recall one day; out of the blue I saw her graduation picture in a photo studio called Zemen around Addis Ababa Municipality Office. Not long afterwards, I found myself in tears for she wore a red lipstick matching her red jumper. I was not very appreciative of ladies who were using make-up at that time. But who am I to approve or disapprove her look in the photo?

The same day, I knelt on my knees and said words of prayer by calling her name to God to bring her in front of me as a wife – this was crazy! Looking back, that was my worst wrong prayer I ever made in light of the word of God. God would not listen to that kind of nonsense. It was not a prayer made according to His will. If I prayed, "Lord, please give me Your grace and favour when I talk to her" could have been a better prayer. He wanted me to go and talk to her. That way He could have helped me in the process. God helps those who help themselves earnestly.

My professor Dr Yacob Arsano Atito could not understand the

puzzle that one of his best students was leaving blank pages only with his name on the exam paper. Henceforth, he wrote an urgent note on the department notice board saying, 'Hello Merid Tadesse Ergicho – Come Immediately to Dr Yacob Arsano's office. I would like to talk to you!' And the note advised any student who read the notice and came across me to inform me that my lecturer was looking for me. After a while, when I met one of my department students, he told me about the notice that Professor Yacob was looking for me as a matter of urgency. I went to his office and found him there. After we exchanged greetings, he said, "Merid – I could not understand how you were not able to answer those questions which gave a freedom of thoughts to explain your own arguments of local administration course. What had happened?"

I had been thinking too much about her during my exam time – the intensity would double or triple. Indeed, I was not properly thinking at all. She would steal my heart and brain. I was in the grip of an obsession of her and powerless to resist thinking about her. Hence, if there was no proper thinking process, there would be nothing to write down. That is how the act of writing works!

I remember the questions were like "Divide Ethiopia into a different regional setting and explain why you would prefer your arrangement over the present way of local administration" type. The other one was "What type of government system do you prefer – federal or unitary system and why?". They were open-ended questions and free for any kind of discussion. Weren't they?

I was one of the students who was tipped to be a junior lecturer in the university by the department teachers and things were not going right? How could somebody avert this invisible force of sight-love into non-existence or to a better evil? I did not develop an infatuation with this young lady. Yes, it was love but sight-love can be an overwhelming sensation that feels like love, though it may not be a true love. It could be an indication of strong physical attraction. This does not mean this person might be a good lifelong match. Although physical attraction is needed for a healthy relationship and to be able to maintain a sexual relationship, more is needed to sustain a long-term relationship.

Thus, I told my professor that I had fallen in love with a student on campus. He asked me, "Which one among the three young ladies in my year, same department?" None of them. In fact, three of them were my good ordinary friends. I had never thought of them in any special way like romantically connected with one of them as they were not able to release joy juice in my body system.

They were beautiful and from well-to-do families. One of them was a daughter of a previous government minister, drives her own luxury car and she dined in Blue Top, expensive restaurants close to our campus. The other young lady was from a successful business family and also dined in the same place. The last one was from a successful and educated family with a decent income.

Then, he said, "Merid, you see, what you had been through is a normal life process. I had confidence in you that you would sort it out. I was in a very difficult position to allocate your grade without knowing what went wrong with you during exam time and I was trying to connect the dots to figure it out but did not succeed until you come to explain it for me." He had those rare qualities of kindness and care to his students which would put him beyond a professional lecturer.

He was one of the most amazing professors that I ever came across in my life even considering the two universities I attended in the UK for my Master's Degree and a Post-graduate Diploma. He was always sensible and non-judgemental! He is also a profound water scientist of Ethiopia and an authority figure in the Nile basin politics with a great comprehension of the politics of the Horn of Africa.

When I was in my final year, my mum told me I would score the highest grades in my studies as the young lady with whom I was in love was graduating. Was that true? In my diary written in 1994, it reads, "Talking about love, I suffered more in her absence than in her presence." May God bless my mum to keep it so long in her heart and discuss it later when she thought it was safer to talk about. A mother full of wisdom, insights and understanding in the society where she lives and beyond.

The young lady whom I had sight-love with had a friend who was studying law. Law was a five-year course. So even if she had left university, she kept her intimate friend with me to remind me of her. The one who was studying law and the young lady with whom I fell in love with were inseparable close friends – they used to go to the Café, Library, outside of the university together that my mind was accustomed to that cycle of life.

Then every single moment I encountered the law student, my brain was projecting the young lady with whom I had fallen in love, next to her. I wonder whether that was a better experience or worse. I should have some psychological counselling which I had never considered before. I should have some kind of cognitive behavioural therapy (CBT) with my situation. I doubt if we had those kinds of professional services around that time in Ethiopia.

In the subjective vision theory of David Friedrich Strauss (1808–1874), in his Life of Jesus (1835), he argued that the resurrection was not an objective historical fact, but a subjective "recollection" of Jesus, transfiguring the dead Jesus into an imaginary, or "mythical," risen Christ. In light of this, hallucinating and projecting the young lady's image next to her friend without her actual presence was possible in my mind. However, she was not a real object as Jesus was physically seen after his death for our sins with his disciples and the two people who were on the road going to a village called

Emmaus, about seven miles from Jerusalem. There is categorical Biblical evidence for the fact that our Lord Jesus has risen. There could not be medical evidence as medical recording was not yet started.

> *"When he was at the table with them, he took bread, gave thanks, broke it and began to give it to them. Then their eyes were opened and they recognised him, and he disappeared from their sight."*
> (Luke 24:30 – 31)

Eventually, a light came to my mind even why I had fallen in love with her. It was unbelievable how the brain faculty works. It was like this – after I finished my high school during summer break, one of my older brothers, Tariku, invited me to stay with him in a place called Enchini. There was this gorgeous young lady called Meraf with whom I used to play a lot – we chased each other on the grass, roll over in the mud and fell down on the bed either in her home or in my brother's home. It was a pure love just to play and have fun – nothing more and nothing less.

One day my brain brought her images from its archive turn by turn in sequence and I was shocked to discover their close resemblance – the young lady with whom I contracted sight-love in the university and the other pretty soul with whom I had moments of great happiness playing with during my stay in my older brother's home. What a coincidence? Thus, I knew my love was rooted because of my previous experience with somebody who looked like her a lot. How does Psychology explain this? I decided to take Psychology and Counselling courses to unearth more details about how love could start in one's life. What are the reasons why we fall in love with someone but not with another person? How are we able to sustain our normal life when a relationship fails?

I would not dare say that my experience of sight-love in the university was a mind fiction. Mind control fiction is a body of literature that includes or is based on the premise that some kind of force is capable of controlling an individual's mind, usually in order to prompt them into some course of action that they normally would not consider.

I let them go . . . Loving them and wishing all the best in their lives. I needed to move on in my life . . . I am writing just for the record.

CHAPTER 4

Broken Promises

How do you see the following true story which happened in Ethiopia in regards to broken relationships? There were a boyfriend and a girlfriend who were worshipping in the Full Gospel Protestant Church in Ethiopia. They stayed in a relationship together for thirteen years – a very long courtship period indeed. They had also exchanged engagement rings ahead of their planned wedding day.

As their wedding day was approaching fast, both families were busy and committed preparing for the great day. When it was only one week away from the Wedding Day the fiancée called her boyfriend on the landline telephone only to tell him that she would not marry him. The boy immediately committed suicide the day he heard his potential wife's final decision to call off the wedding. The two of them had attended marriage lessons together in their church. There was no indication from the girl that she would not marry him in their thirteen years of romantic relationships or even when they attended the marriage lessons.

The boyfriend was an evangelist who was ministering in the countryside branch churches. It must have been heart-breaking for the boyfriend to reach that decision of taking his own life. I am not judging him but it would have been better and happier if he had decided to let her go. There could be somebody else who would love to live with him. *"Yet you, LORD, are our father. We are the clay; you are the potter; we are all the work of your hand. Do not be angry beyond measure, LORD; do not remember our sins forever. Oh, look on us, we pray, for we are all your people."* (Isaiah 64:8-9)

Losing brilliant academic opportunities and scoring an "F" in a course could be okay because of sight or romantic love like me. Why would you kill yourself for someone refusing to marry you? There is always somebody out there who is the right one for you to start the journey of life. It is good to have a great belief that you start and finish the married life together. There are no stations in the middle of the trip and be sure you travel to the end of the journey. Beautiful end. Choose the right bricks which are long-lasting as you will be in several treacherous storms which you could be fighting together with the Power of God (POG). I chose one as you read my story.

Once there was a minor earthquake when I was in Asmara University in the late 1980s. We were in a classroom learning Chemistry and we felt the earthquake and had seen some of its effects, like the desks and chairs shaking. Some of my classmates ran to the glass windows to break them and jump down to the ground from the third-floor of the building. Our lecturer stopped them saying, "Don't damage yourselves before nature damages you!" Likewise, when somebody prefers to withdraw from a love relationship that could be a fatal incident in your lives. But, let the serious storms ebb away from your life. If I did it, you could do it better. Let those difficult days go. Someone better may come into your life if you hoped and kept on praying. When God closes the door, look through the window – His blessings are the best!

Suicide is a grave sin equivalent to murder (Exodus 20:13; 21:23), but it can be forgiven like any other sin. And Scripture says clearly that those redeemed by God have been forgiven for all their sins – past, present, and future (Colossians 2: 13 – 14). Paul says in Romans 8: 38 – 39 that nothing can separate us from the love of God in Christ Jesus. So, if a true Christian would commit suicide in a time of extreme weakness, he or she would be received into heaven (Jude 24). But we question the faith of those who take their lives or even consider it seriously – it may well be that they have never been truly saved.

That's because God's children are defined repeatedly in Scripture as those who have hope (Acts 24:15; Romans 5: 2 – 5, 8:24; 2 Corinthians 1:10, etc) and purpose in life (Luke 9:23 – 25; Romans 8: 28; Colossians 1:29). And those who think of committing suicide do so because they have neither hope nor purpose in their lives.

Furthermore, one who repeatedly considers suicide is practising sin in his heart (Proverbs 23:7), and (1 John 3:9) says that "no one who is born of God practices sin." And finally, suicide is often the ultimate evidence of a heart that rejects the lordship of Jesus Christ, because it is an act where the sinner is taking his life into his own hands completely rather than submitting to God's will for it. Surely many of those who have taken their lives will hear those horrifying words from the Lord Jesus at the judgment-"I never knew you; Depart from me, you who practice lawlessness" (Matthew 7:23).

So, though it may be possible for a true believer to commit suicide, we believe that is an unusual occurrence. Someone considering suicide should be challenged above all to examine herself/himself to see whether she/he is in the faith (2 Corinthians 13:5). (3)

On a separate positive note, how about the Ethiopian woman who told me her story when I was working in the Ethiopian Embassy in London.

She said that over fifteen years ago someone had processed a marriage visa for her to come to Germany. She had never met him in person – she had never seen him physically before and hence did not know him at all except probably through the phone. She did not tell me about having telephone conversations – on that I am just making a clever guess. He sent the forms and every necessary documentation and after everything was finalised, she was granted with the appropriate visa to travel to Germany and settle with him.

Mind you, she agreed to proceed with the process because she wanted to go abroad for a better life. Who would not want a better life? Obviously, travelling expesnses were covered by him and she was on board the plane to Berlin, Germany. At the airport, twenty of his male friends, himself and his sister welcomed her. They went home for the celebration of the arrival of the bride for a wedding feast. Besides, she did not have any clue as to who was her actual husband-to-be from the many males who welcomed and accompanied her.

At the end of the celebration, the gentlemen started to leave one by one. Whenever every single one of them was leaving, she was thinking in her heart that this was not the one who would be her husband. Eventually, the last person who remained with her and his sister was a dwarf. She did not expect him at all, that he would be the one marrying her or who was her husband. It was a pity that the bride did not know the bridegroom until then.

The very day she arrived in Berlin she became a fugitive in a city where she had no clue what to do. Suddenly an idea came to her mind about asking the whereabouts of the Ethiopian Embassy on the streets of Berlin. Eventually, with the best of luck and the direction of helpful people, she found out the address and managed to go there. She told her story to the diplomats who had been working in the Embassy and asked for help to stay with them.

The Ethiopian embassies abroad, as such they did not have provisions for these kinds of emergencies. One guy who was work- ing in the Embassy volunteered to offer her a room in his own accommodation as he was single. After some time, they started dating each other and became special friends. Later she willingly cohabited with him until he sent her to the UK. Do you know that cohabiting couples are separating at the rate of 60-70% in the developed world? She told me that she had a really good time with the diplomat and he finally helped her with the visa process to travel to the UK.

Below is another story about an Adventist young lady in Addis Ababa whose beauty was second to none. Anybody who came across her could easily be attracted to her beauty. She was very attractive with a pleasant personality. Thus, a young man who was from the same church as her asked her for a date. To his surprise, she agreed and gave him details of her address and invited him to come over to her apartment. He came on time and they chatted for so long and he told her that he was feeling love towards her. "That's fine with me," she said. "But," she enquired, "are you sure about your love?"

"Absolutely, yes!" was his answer.

She served him tea with some biscuits and they chilled-out on the balcony. Then, the moment of truth had come. As he was looking at her in wonder, she unbuttoned her white shirt to the bottom to expose part of her body. She showed him the huge scars under her breast on her belly which was burned by fire when she was a young age. She openly showed him so that he could have a good understanding of her unseen physical appearance – especially the one which was covered by a cloth. The hidden one where he could not see . . .

The guy did not come back again. Did he truly feel love towards her? He could have been. However, is love only a feeling? I really doubt it. Love should not be only feelings as my undergraduate university friend Deka from Sudan, used to say, "Love needs to be practical – something which you could put it into action." When the feelings of love go, if someone did not have what it takes to be committed to her/his marriage, then everything will be futile. You need an anchor here – the trust, responsibility, patience, commitment, knowledge, wisdom, insights, goodness, kindness, etc. Love is beyond feeling. Jesus kept it simple. He taught and demonstrated that love is an action. As John explains, *"Let us not love in word or in tongue, but indeed and in truth"* (1 John 3:18).

As she kept on narrating her own story to me, she told me that she had encountered another person who was singing her a love song – about her beauty and their lives together. He sang, "I am that little robin, that sits upon a tree. I sing to you each morning, but you don't know it is me. I am that little robin, in your garden every day, I will never leave you, I will never fly away." The other poem was, "When things get tough you may feel you are on your own but I am here for you and you are not alone. Try to hang in there and take things day by day and anytime you need me I will be with you all the way." After all those songs and poems, he was invited to her apartment like the first one, to have a reality check. Did he pass it? Absolutely not!

The third gentleman, a true Christian, came into her life who later became her husband. This one, as he had genuine guidance by the Holy Spirit, when she was about to unbutton her shirt, he told her: "Please do not be bothered to show me a part of your body which was burned and left a scar on your body as God already revealed it to me in my dream and vision about you." They got married and were blessed with a happy family, raising their three children at the time the woman told me her own story, about thirty-three years ago. Dreams and visions are the languages of Holy Spirit and the God Most High helped her to find a reliable brick. God knows how to find you the right one if you involve Him in every aspect of your life. He is available and willing to help! He is Faithful!

How about the gentleman who married a woman with a skin disease? He had never seen her body before the wedding night and as he discovered it – he noted that would be his prayer topic about his wife. He kept on praying and after sometime he found out that her skin was changed to a shiny, beautiful skin like a newborn baby. God answers prayers when we live a righteous life according to His word.

Did you also hear about the lady who married a Christian husband but had never cooked in her life? The wedding gifts from her parents were seven books on how to cook, thereby deliberately informing him that she could not cook. A diplomatic way of saying, "Please understand that she was not trained how to cook and let it not be a cause for an argument in your marriage." The next day, the husband threw six of the cookery books through the window, boosting his new wife's confidence and they started cooking together with the one book that they chose to keep. Later, he witnessed his wife became the best cook in the whole wide world even the meals prepared in the palaces would not compare with the succulent and scrumptious food she prepares. Look at the differences encouraging people could bring to your life.

As you can read and see, the last three paragraphs are unbroken promises made by people and God helped them to live by their words. The saying goes, "Unless your promise is a promise, do not promise a promise." It is interesting to compare and contrast how our lives will be when people whom we know make and break their promises in our daily life. How challenging is it?

CHAPTER 5

ZEBIDAR's Democracy and Diplomacy

"The LORD said to Moses, "Come up to me on the mountain and stay here, and I will give you the tablets of stone with the law and commandments I have written for their instruction." (Exodus 24:12)

What is the first thing which comes to your mind when you think of the ZEBIDAR Mountains? That they are in chains of beautiful mountains. Yes, absolutely RIGHT. The massif mountains could have piled up one on the top of another during creation with His Majesty's goodwill and became one of the tallest mountains on the planet.

Instead, when they were created, the Creator thought they should be in chains to show us unity, tolerance and peaceful co-existence. They dismissed selfish individuality for mass embracing great values of SHARING. The Zebidar mountains seem to understand the British values for schools well ahead of time. For schools in the UK, British values refers to a set of values that the government believes learning those values are important for children. They include respect for the rule of law, individual liberty, democracy, and mutual respect for and tolerance of different faiths and beliefs.

In today's world, people found out the principles of respecting one another very difficult with their selfish attitude. And people assert that self-centredness is the biggest privilege given to humankind, but we use it less and less in this modern society. The ZEBIDAR Chains of Mountains got the golden principles of respecting one another fascinatingly attractive for several millenniums. They also discovered peaceful co-existence as the best way of living.

As human-beings, who are created in the image and likeness of God, we will be blessed and more astounding to live together loving one another. How did we fail to learn love and respect from the mountains – ZEBIDAR's democracy?

On a separate positive note, I would like to happily introduce and share a few catchphrases about 'Shepherd's Diplomacy' and its own love potion which is called CHIKO.

The Shepherd

This traditional luxurious dessert after a meal in Ethiopia, CHIKO, has its own vital role as an instrument of personal diplomacy. My magnanimous mother used to prepare me home-made chiko of the best quality, which I shared with some ambassadors and diplomats of other countries. If not thousands or hundreds, tens of diplomats and ambassadors eagerly tasted it and they fell in love with our rich food cultures. **Thank you, my mother, Worknesh Woldemariam Melsebo, the most wonderful mother someone could ever wish to have, I am richly blessed to have you as my marvellous mother.**

It sounds crazy. BUT love knows no law and boundary. Sometimes you have to forget the 'health and safety' rules or standards, or in other words take risks when I encouraged diplomats to enjoy the delicious chiko. Love always wins! GOD is LOVE. *"Love is patient, love is kind. It does not envy, it does not boast, it is not proud. It does not dishonour others, it is not self-seeking, it is not easily angered, it keeps no record of wrongs. Love does not delight in evil but rejoices with the truth. It always protects, always trusts, always hopes, always perseveres. Love never fails. But where there are prophecies, they will cease; where there are tongues, they will be stilled; where there is knowledge, it will pass away."* (1 Corinthians 13:4 – 8)

Let me cast a light upon this new concept called 'Shepherd's Diplomacy'. Shepherd's diplomacy (a catchphrase coined by myself for future texts in foreign policy and the diplomatic arena) is a lower level of diplomacy which involves management of international relations, the art of dealing with people in a sensitive and tactful way predominantly by winning people's hearts with care and love.

The whole idea of shepherd's diplomacy is to bring people in general and diplomats in particular to the world you represent (creating a positive and peaceful attitude and solidarity towards your government and country).

It is always propitious to tackle a lower-level diplomatic crisis before it escalates and becomes a state issue. It is usually handled by junior diplomatic staff who strive for excellence as an important part of professionalism. Thus, it will save the time, energy and resources of senior personnel in government affairs, foreign policy and diplomacy.

Practical Scenario – Case Study:

In the year 1999, a diplomat of Ivory coast/Cote d'Ivoire, one of the West African countries, wanted to get access to the passengers' hall of Bole International Addis Ababa Airport to check-in his ambassador's luggage with the Ethiopian Airlines flight to Abidjan. At the time, some of the Airport Police were not good at conversing in spoken English. Thus, they physically blocked him from entering the hall to inform him that he was not allowed to enter the gate as he was not a passenger. The airport police fell short in verbally explaining what he should have done. Body language sometimes has its own limitations as it may not be able to explain the next few steps. The airport police physically pushing anybody, for that matter, was an awkward action from our side of the equation in terms of advising the diplomats what they should do.

Next, the misunderstanding and miscommunication escalated even more to the level of physical abuse. Reports say the diplomat was so frustrated that he pushed one of the policemen who was holding his jacket in the fight – "I needed to get inside the passengers' hall to check-in for my ambassador and 'no you couldn't as you were not a traveller'." Next, the policeman punched the diplomat in the face, smashing his glasses. That was a severe physical assault which was tantamount to committing a criminal offence in the eyes of law in the UK. A physical assault is when an individual or a group attacks a person physically, with or without the use of a weapon, or threatens to hurt that person. It can include scratching, pushing, kicking, punching, throwing things, using weapons or physically restraining another person.

Solution:

People who work in and around airports should be trained in international spoken and written languages to alleviate these sorts of problems, or else a signpost with a text of "Restricted Access Only to Passengers" could have been enough information to avoid unnecessary disputes. I am not sure whether these kind of helpful pieces of information are given due attention at the present time or not. However, that we did not have these simple signposts at the time damaged our reputation as a government and they brought about an abominable image of the country.

In this case, the policemen were expected to explain to the diplomat that there was another gateway to get into the passengers' hall for the checking-in process, after being checked in a walk-through as a security precaution. This gate allowed people who were accompanying or facilitating passengers' travels but who do not travel themselves. The security assumption is that people who were not travelling could bring some security risks to passengers in the passenger hall if they are allowed to get into the hall without being checked and could exit for their safety. Whereas passengers did not have that choice of leaving the hall once they checked in – it made perfect sense!

Hence, people who facilitate other passengers' journeys used to be checked thoroughly before they were allowed to get into the passengers' hall. The diplomat might have not been aware that that kind of rules and facilities existed, especially if he was a new diplomat. Moreover, the policemen should have been able to inform and explain to the diplomat about those provisions, but they were not able to do that as they couldn't speak English.

Nevertheless, this was a real case scenario which had escalated to the level of the two heads of governments, namely the then Ethiopian Prime Minister and the Ivory Coast President at the time. I recall, the Ivory Coast President had summoned the ambassador of Ethiopia in Abidjan, Ambassador Wosen Beshah. Ivory Coast had demanded a full detailed report about that very incident (why his diplomats were in official protest against the host country, Addis Ababa – Ethiopia) which could have been dealt with at low-level diplomacy. In other words, the skills of shepherd's diplomacy could have fully resolved it.

The officer in charge who could have resolved this outstanding problem at that time did not have the skill to alleviate the problem and things swiftly made wrong-turns. It should have been resolved on the spot! The Ethiopian Ministry of Foreign Affairs established an ad hoc committee which involved me to study and investigate the case and report to the General Director of Protocol and the General Director to the late Minister of Foreign Affairs, H.E. Mr Seyoum Mesfin, who in turn would report to the late Prime Minister, H.E. Meles Zenawi.

Cote d'Ivoire diplomats campaigned against Ethiopia to take away Ethiopia's privilege of having the Headquarters of the Organisation of African Union (OAU), presently known as African Unity (AU), for the host country was not treating African diplomats respectfully according to their views. They succeeded in mobilising some other African countries who were not happy at the time. Diplomatic hostility could easily spread out like a wildfire if host countries are not careful in handling them.

We needed to be realistic, apologetic and patient with the unfriendly wave of diplomatic underground riots by other countries which usually was manifested in getting angry and upset so quickly in the fulfilment of all their demands by the host country, Ethiopia. Later, the upheaval went down through time with a lot of determined effort and good gestures on our side.

As you can see from the above scenario, you do not need to go to Harvard, Oxford or any other highly prestigious academic universities to be a shepherd. You will be a good shepherd through experience and a keen heart to do the right things. Of course, you need both written and spoken language skills in English and that does require a lot of knowledge.

Shepherds look after their flocks and herds to good pastures. Naturally, flocks and herds do not complain to their senior superiors that their shepherds did not treat them well. As a matter of fact, the shepherd is the highest hierarchy in terms of authority in the chain-of-command. Nonetheless, the question that remains to be answered is – are all shepherds good and caring? Do they fight back if an enemy comes to hurt one of their flock or will they run to save their own lives? Are all of them equipped with negotiation skills and wisdom in the management of public and international affairs to resolve outstanding problems? As to the negotiation skills, you may need as little as a practical experience mentioned below.

At the age of nine, I went to the open market, shops, bars and bus stations to sell kolo and contribute to the family's income. (Kolo – one type could be made using barley by removing the two outer layers and lightly broiling them and then mix with the other seeds like nuts, peas, chickpeas for flavour.) I was very successful not only as a kolo seller but also as a gifted negotiator. How? There was this notorious and fearless boy called Chirih around Hosana Buna Bet or Restaurant, where we used to sell massive amount of kolo as there were several hundreds of passengers going to and from Hosana to Addis Ababa. He put an embargo on some of us so that we were not able to go and sell in that busy centre. At that point, I even thought of forming "Kolo Sellers Association" as I did believe "Unity was/is Strength"!

Later, I negotiated with him that we would be giving him ten cents kolo as tax to get access to the vicinity every day. He was the most irresponsible boy that I had ever known. I saw him pushing kolo sellers and their kolo spilling over on the ground. People who did not hold responsibilities in their lives seemed to care less about what they do.

Mind you, by the same token, some diplomats wanted to exercise a form of excessive legal immunity – diplomatic immunity out of its scope, and abuse the Vienna Convention of 1961 on Diplomatic Relations. The international agreements on diplomatic immunity can be found in the Vienna Convention on Diplomatic Relations. For instance, **the receiving state is not permitted to prosecute diplomats, and must protect them, along with their families and property**. In light of this, I recall, a charged affaire of the Equatorial Guinea (I remember his name but prefer not to mention it) came to my office and stood by the door. I could tell he was angry by the look of him and the tone of his voice.

He commanded, "Mr Merid – come here!" I did not hesitate; I went closer to him to see what he was going to do. He raised up his foot and forcefully landed it on mine and cried out, "This was the way your policeman mistreated me by the entrance of the VIP lounge for I went inside to check whether the wife of my ambassador was inside the lounge or not." I humbly said to the diplomat, "Sir, sometimes words could explain incidents better than actions. You should have explained it to me orally than stomping on me." Stepping on somebody's feet is not included in the provision of the Vienna Convention of Diplomatic Rights, neither accusing a policeman who was on duty and demanding what the procedure dictated. The diplomat should have presented a VIP Permission Paper or got assistance from me or the Airport Security Office to get access in times of emergency. He had failed to do all the three options which were available to him.

What is diplomatic immunity? Diplomatic immunity is a principle of international law by which certain foreign government officials are not subject to the jurisdiction of local courts and other authorities for both their official and, to a large extent, their personal activities. In this particular case, the diplomat was at fault and acted irresponsibly and insensibly. As a result, he regretted with his wrong deeds and came to me for apologies the next day with a card on which he wrote a "sorry" message and two black level whiskies. Apology accepted in the highest consideration of the national interest of my country.

Selling kolo had taught me to be duty-minded, take responsibility, be patient, love and share with other people. It was an invaluable experience and gave me the wisdom to subtly and skilfully handle difficult situations, including my own marriage. In conclusion, as a host country, we were always mindful of international conventions and protocols. If you like ETHIOPIA, ETHIOPIA likes you back! The law should serve everyone equally and must be universally applicable. Sometimes, problems could happen anywhere in the globe – we need to find an amicable solution which works for all parties involved. We need to be solution-oriented and peace-makers to the stability and peace of this beautiful, big earth.

Practice Point:

- Do you think the diplomatic rights and privileges of diplomats should be amended or changed?
- If you are interested to read more about the 1961 Vienna Convention on Diplomatic Relations, the internet can be very helpful.

CHAPTER 6

Zebidar Airport

The streets of London were all illuminated by strong, eye-catching lights, that made the shepherd's life an uneasy one at the beginning. He was not used to this kind of lifestyle – shepherd diplomat. He went to Prince Albert and Tower Bridges several times to wonder how the engineers constructed them. He had also been to the different Royal Parks, like Hyde Park and Regent's Park, and wished he could bring his flocks of sheep from Ethiopia. His sheep knew his voice, especially the ones by the bottom of the Chain Mountains – ZEBIDAR.

His way of life was – waking up at dawn (before the first light of the day came) and taking his herds and flocks to the bottom of the mountains where there were plenty of pastures, and at dusk (when the last light of the day went) he returned to his hut with his loved ones (animals and children). He could then pray and sleep. It was a simple, happy and peaceful life. No cases of human rights, diplomacy, foreign policy and politics involved in it.

The shepherd was full of love – he got it from the Love-Chains of Mountains – ZEBIDAR. In the old golden days when he was quite young, he sat down at the bottom of Zebidar and looked proudly to his happy flocks and herds which were enjoying the grazing lush pastures. That was his perfect world! Now that his life has changed, he hallucinated a lot about his cattle, ZEBIDAR and the nearby magnificent meadows with rabbits running around them.

Last Saturday around lunchtime, he left his home in Battersea for a long walk looking for a serene place like ZEBIDAR. He walked and walked, passing through several blocks. As he got closer to the big buildings, they lit up with their sensor fluorescent lights and outdoor bulbs. The buildings were not secured as much as the people who were living in them, he wondered. They were not fully fenced.

Hours later, he found himself in the suburbs, in a small village, completely exhausted. Nevertheless, his mind freshened up with the quietness of the area. It was dreadfully dark. He put on his torch to look around, swept the ground with his old jacket and lay down using a big stone as a pillow.

Instantly, he was in a deep sleep.

That evening, he visualised ZEBIDAR growing or shrinking at will. One moment he was an enormous man and the next, the size of a blade of grass. After a while Zebidar turned himself into an enormous man, got closer to the shepherd and ran his big fingers up-and-down on the shepherd's body, especially under his armpit. In his slumber, the shepherd muttered, "It tickles. Ha ha ha . . . Who are you?" He was not fully awake.

It is me – ZEBIDAR. "Why are you so afraid to write down about my future project – ZEBIDAR AIRPORT IN BUTAJIRA (ZAB)?" furiously enquired Zebidar.

The shepherd had attempted to rationalise in regards to this future project of building ZEBIDAR AIRPORT TERMINAL in Butajira early on. Airport Terminals and runway construction need an enormous amount of space. On the other hand, airports bring sound and air pollutions to the environment. Who will also give up the grazing pastures and the farming lands to the fulfilment of what ZEBIDAR was asking for? It is also a big investment. Who was going to finance it all?

The straight and levelled lands around Mekicho, Ticho, Koto, Kela, Dobi or other places are ideal for airport construction so they say. Nonetheless, they are the livelihoods of the farmers' households and local residents in those areas.

You know, in the past, the shepherd did not dare speak straight to ZEBIDAR. But then, he had gotten the guts to confront him to explain why the local airport was needed.

Zebidar firmly said, "Just write down the idea and pass it on to the next generation. A time will come when other people wish to continue from where you stopped. You know me well, my son. 'I am an advocate of continuity.' Always starting from scratch is energy, time and resource consuming." Eventually, Zebidar promised that my own great-grandchildren will take direct flights from Europe and America to Butajira Airport. So did other people of the region. Moreover, visitors from every corner of the world will enjoy these direct flights to ZEBIDAR.

Wasn't our Smoking-Chains of Mountains – ZEBIDAR, super intelligent?

It won't be long before people in the globe will be fed up with going to the beaches for recreation. You see, my son; they will need a substitute – a mountain camping holiday for a beach holiday. Did you notice how the social media and electronic gadgets/games had changed families and societal values around the world? Change is inevitable – it is right under your nose?

One day, people all over the world will make mountain biking, climbing and hiking their principal holiday activities. Thus, if we are ready with the different options of transportations, we could benefit from it.

"Is that it?" the shepherd demanded.

"What do you mean? This is the best answer you would get," Zebidar replied.

Then, the shepherd woke up from his dream. What a beautiful dream it was!

The shepherd now loves ZEBIDAR more than anything. Anything except Glorious God who gave Zebidar to the people of this town! Butajira will have its own airport in the future as the country's economy developed and diversified into several sectors. Someone does not need to be a rocket scientist to make this kind of bold statement if people are praying with faith and expectancy and working hard to achieve their goals (GOAL – Ground Operations Aerospace Language). The law of nature also states that things grow from simple to more complex and from small to large. Butajira follows a similar pattern – from being a small town to a great city like Battersea Town or Boston!

Praying with faith and expectancy will always attract the presence and power of God. There is a direct correlation between the level of belief and expectancy in the hearts of people and the measure of the revelation of the glory of God. When God's people pray in the firm conviction that it is God's will to answer their prayers and reveal His glory, their expectation of His glory will bring its manifestations in their lives. This is my piece of advice to the people of Butajira and beyond. Please read the story below.

Many years ago, a region of the American Midwest had been stricken by drought. There was a small town there that was totally dependent upon farming, and the crops were dying in the fields because of the lack of rain. A day of prayer and fasting was declared in which all the townspeople would come in from their surrounding farms and spend the day in prayers, asking God to send rain.

That morning a five-year-old girl came along with her parents to their church to pray. Some people were amused as this little girl was carrying an umbrella. They asked her why. She replied that she thought they had come there that day to pray for rain, and she did not want to get wet going home.

Suddenly conviction gripped their hearts. The people realised that they had come to pray, yet no one but this little girl actually believed anything was going to change! In tears, they repented of their unbelief; and these same townspeople began to pray that day as though they really believed their prayers were going to change things.

About four o'clock that afternoon, clouds began to form on the western sky. By the evening, a slow soaking rain had begun to fall across the region. The Heavens had literally opened for these people. This slow rain lasted for three days and nights. Their crops were saved, and they eventually had one of the biggest harvests that they had ever seen! Everyone remembered that it was the little girl with the umbrella who had come to pray and had changed their hearts from a place of religious duty bound with unbelief to a place of expectancy that God would in fact hear and act.

We must believe and expect God's best blessings whenever we pray. Prayer is the key that unlocks the doors that man tries to keep closed. Zebidar believes in prayer and certain things need prayers for decades. Some centuries. So, pray that Butajira will have its own airport – Zebidar Airport of Butajira (ZAB) for the future generations.

CHAPTER 7

Zebidar – The Flying Mountains!

The sun was rising in the sky. The shepherd muttered, "La ilaha illallah!" (There is no god but God) not believing what he was looking at.

One moment it was standing upright on its hind legs, and then it locked its stretched ends together. At first it walked and a bit later rolled like a hoop towards the main road of Butajira in the direction of Addis Ababa, the capital city of Ethiopia.

The shepherd did not know what to do and could not believe his eyes. "Was I dreaming about Zebidar like any other times before?" he asked himself and instantly answered (to himself) "No, I was not dreaming. It was real."

He rubbed his eyes twice to make sure it wasn't a dream. As wings sprouted from Zebidar's shoulders, I knew it was going to fly. Then, it was impossible to follow as it disappeared out of my sight. I shivered, as fear like ice spread through my body. I knew a sighting of Zebidar Mountains flying was an omen of death.

Almost at once it flew back at an incredible speed and said, "Do not ever be afraid. I am one of your great, great, great forefathers. We are connected with a strong bond. Take delight in doing good and peaceful things."

Zebidar further advised, "When people tell you their problems, carry their burden with them. Try to stand on their side and appreciate their problems as yours. Pray and push their problems to the best of your ability and knowledge until a time comes, they are free from their problems. Be helpful and ask for help whenever you need one." There is one famous saying of the National Health Service (NHS) in the UK – "Help us to help you!"

Slowly, the rapid beat of my heart became calmer and my pale face relaxed, as the tension in my body eased. Later, I politely thanked, "Oh, Zebidar, Majestic Chains of Mountains, thank you for your kindness to come and assure me that I was safe and wouldn't die of looking at you flying."

Zebidar laughed a big, hearty laugh like the one it previously did in London for its visit on my wedding day – Saturday, July 13th 2003. The laughter echoed from one end of that great town of Butajira to the other end and it stated, "I am going to the Ministry of Education of Ethiopia, Addis Ababa."

Abruptly, it flew with the speed of light – a speed impossible to track. Nothing can travel faster than 300,000 kilometres per second (186,000 miles per second). Only massless particles, including photons, which make up light, can travel at that speed. Itʋs impossible to accelerate any material object up to the speed of light because it would take an infinite amount of energy to do so. Nonetheless, Zebidar defied that scientific fact and convention. Zebidar flew with the speed of light!

Practice Point:

- Why do you think Zebidar Chains of Mountains preferred flying to walking to Addis Ababa?
- Why do you think Zebidar wanted to visit the Ministry of Education?
- Email your answers to mergicho@gmail.com

The people of Butajira came out of their homes from every corner hearing the big, hearty laughter of Zebidar which echoed from one end to the other. They looked around in wonder and could not see the graceful Chains of Mountains – Zebidar.

It was an eerie experience! Huge black clouds blocked out the sun, and darkness fell early in the morning instead of bright, glorious light. The earth trembled, shook the ground and sent everything downwards.

After a while, the shepherd shouted out loud to the people on a microphone, "People of Butajira, do not be afraid! I brought you some great news with me. Our Majestic Chains of Mountains – Zebidar will be back soon with success." The people enquired, "Who are you? We do not even know you! How can we trust you?" Before he said a word, some of the elderly people went closer to the shepherd and smelled him thoroughly. They exclaimed, "He smells like us. He must be one of our lost sons. Welcome home!" Then, they gave him a loving look and hugged him tightly and affectionately.

On the other hand, Zebidar landed quietly like a cat right in front of the Ministry of Education, Addis Ababa. Not to disrupt the traffic in the city, it used its hind legs to stand. To the surprise of humankind in the 21st century, local and international mountains delegates came to show their solidarity and gave support to Zebidar's Proposal. All the mountains stood gracefully on both sides of Zebidar. On its right was Mount Kilimanjaro and on its left among so many others was Mount Everest.

They were dancing and chanting, "Zebidar deserves to be in the National Curricula of Ethiopia. We support this brilliant idea! Be proud of your own treasures! Most Ethiopian children know about Kilimanjaro and Everest Mountains but not about Zebidar . . ."

"The mountains danced like sheep and the hills like little lambs." (Psalms 114:4)

Zebidar kindly demanded to talk to the Curriculum Director in the Ministry of Education of Ethiopia. A kind-looking gentleman came out of the building and asked, "How may I help you (Zebidar), please? I am the Education Minister, Dr Berhanu Nega." Zebidar was surprised with the unexpected reception he got. He pressed the palms of his hands against his chin and gazed into the distance. His face turned soft and sympathetic and his voice sank to a murmur. Eventually, he cleared his throat and announced, **"Minister, thank you for your time to come and see me. May you please include me in THE NATIONAL CURRICULUM OF ETHIOPIAN EDUCATION?"**

The education minister listened carefully, his head tilted and his brow furrowed with concentration. Next, he flashed a comforting smile and attested that **Zebidar – the Majestic Chains of Guraghe Mountains will soon be included in the education system. Every child will learn about Zebidar Chains of Mountains and even school trips will be arranged with the budget of the Ministry of Education to those schools which show interest and have the**

capacity to do so. The education minister made a huge promise to Zebidar. The local as well as the international Mountains Delegates jubilantly jumped up and down with the greatest news their friend Zebidar had received. At once, the news was covered by Ethiopian Broadcasting Service (EBS), British Broadcasting Corporation (BBC), Cable News Network (CNN) and other major international news agencies alongside social media. The news went viral!

The Mountains Delegates flew back to their original places peacefully and safely.

Zebidar flew back, stretched its ends and a rainbow appeared in the sky. From every hill came the gurgling of water – the music of invisible fountains as the rivers tumbled down the slopes. *"Whenever the rainbow appears in the clouds, I will see it and remember the everlasting covenant between God and all living creatures of every kind on the earth."* So, God said to Noah, *"This is the sign of the covenant I have established between me and all life on earth."* (Genesis 9: 16 -17)

The people suddenly started to chant, "Zebidar, Zebidar, Zebidar – Our treasure. Our gift from Sovereign and Supreme God. Our precious possession from Mighty God. You are our beauty and we love you . . ."

CHAPTER 8

Talking Rivers!

"Let the rivers clap their hands, let the mountains sing together for joy; let them sing before the LORD, for he comes to judge the earth. He will judge the world in righteousness and the peoples with equity." (Psalm 98:8)

As the sun rose, the sky changed to orange and then red. Millions of sparkles like diamonds burst out onto Erenzaf River, making the water dance and shimmer. The swimming ducks and their ducklings on the river gave a magnificent beauty to the surroundings. "What a terrific day!" exclaimed a shepherd who was crossing by.

A little bit further down from Erenzaf River bridge, closer to 'Arategna Bahir' (Amharic name given to that specific spot of the river for its deep-end), birds moved in the treetops, branches swayed and leaves rustled as nature greeted the sun and the new day. I moved my flocks of sheep and herds of cattle towards the direction of the Camp, planning our way to Shershera (the name of a countryside village where there were pastures). I took them further away to the bottom of the Evergreen and Gleeful Zebidar Chains of Mountains.

The Camp is like an ancient city of Jericho which was fenced by walls and the people who inhabited it were highway construction workers, families and their heavy machineries of every sort. By the way, it was not open to outsiders. I met my big brother's friend, Mr Tilahun Tezera, who was privileged to live there and talked about it in fond memories of childhood. We were by the beach in Littlehampton, West Sussex for a Christian families dine-and-worship get-together. The invitation to attend the programme was extended to me from my couple friends Girmay Tesfazgi and Meseret Baysa. Thank you so much for remembering me and may Almighty God remember you for something good. As I always say, "It was not a coincidence for me to be there and Supreme God planned it even before I was born."

As we were leading our (my herds, flocks and I) way, all of a sudden, layers of pregnant clouds clung and blanketed the nearby forest. Then, there was a steady downpour of rain crashing to earth and spreading darkness and damp. The downpour flooded Ufaro River (a little intermittent river which flows in rainy seasons) to overflow and it was galloping with its top speed.

Something unusual caught my attention. I saw and heard the following incident unfolding. Ufaro River was miserably arguing with Erenzaf River. It was complaining about its pace at the confluence of the two rivers.

Ufaro River snarled, "You slowcoach! Can't you move a bit faster and leave a space for me?" Erenzaf River clicked its tongue impatiently and shrugged its shoulders. Muttering under its breath, "This intermittent (seasonal) river has a big mouth! For goodness' sake, it doesn't know what it is doing."

Eyes ablaze, fists clenched, Ufaro hissed at Erenzaf out of the side of its mouth spraying spittle as it spat out the words. In return, Erenzaf was waving its arms wildly in the air, it shrieked at Ufaro and advanced, with bulging eyes in its twisted face.

This is a pure power struggle between the two rivers! Who is bigger or faster instead of who will be serving the communities in their best interests. News travels faster than a wildfire that the inhabitants of Butajira heard all about the two rivers' quarrel and felt heartbroken.

Eresha, another river of Butajira also heard about their squabbles. As Eresha River listened to the news from the shepherd, a troubled expression settled on its face. Next, throwing its head back, it exhaled deeply and closed its eyes and started to think what should be done. Eresha had a problem-solving attitude whenever conflictual interests occur.

Problem-solving orientation refers to one's attitude toward or general approach in dealing with problems and involves emotional and intellectual aspects. Being solution-oriented means, you won't sleep until you help find the answer and/or fix a problem. Solution-oriented people don't just solve problems, they help identify the source of a question or challenge, and provide the right, or a better, way of doing things. Do you think you are one of them?

The shepherd opened his mouth again to speak, but before he could utter a word, Eresha River silenced him by putting its hand, palm upwards, in the air in front of him.

Then, Eresha thoughtfully suggested, "As you were at the scene of the conflict, why do you not try all your best to amicably settle their differences?" The shepherd felt uneasy. He felt terribly depressed about Erenzaf-Ufaro Rivers insulting each other. He knows it is only when they settle down that his flocks of sheep and herds of cattle will quench their thirst.

Then, he went to the rivers and said, "It's the simple things in life that are the most extraordinary. I know how to look after my flocks and herds. When they feel hungry, I will take them to their pastures. When they are thirsty, I drive them to the rivers – to you. I do those simple things which are extraordinary. However, I am not as wise and, in any position, to judge over your conflicting interests. Thus, I will send you to Zebidar Chains of Mountains which are the wisest and most understanding." With the shepherd's suggestion Erenzaf and Ufaro agreed to be judged by ZEBIDAR.

Then, Erenzaf and Ufaro rivers travelled all the way to Majestic Zebidar against their natural course to receive their verdict. Zebidar, the father of social and restorative justices contemplated and said, "Look at the people of Butajira – Muslims and Christians alike – they live in total peace and harmony helping one another. When the Muslims built their mosque the Christians' financial contributions were great and when the Orthodox Christians built the big St Mary Church the Muslims' financial contributions were immense. They deemed to understand one another's perspectives and live in peaceful coexistence. Rivers, when you flow together, you are more graceful. Enjoy each other's perspectives and embrace one another in your lives. Do not ever believe in using force. Love each other! Live with patience as it is a virtue and one of the fruits of God's Spirit."

Zebidar politely asked, "Did you understand me?" And further added, "Unity is strength. May you (Erenzaf and Ufaro Rivers) please DO NOT forget this – I am the source for both of you including Eresha River." They felt ashamed for not being understanding to each other. Eventually, they hugged, clapped, danced and gave their heartfelt huge 'Thank you!' to Zebidar, their mother, and flew gracefully together. The people of Butajira were elated but the shepherd was the one who deeply appreciated their peaceful settlement.

The above was a political literature I wrote about the power struggle of the different political parties in Ethiopia around 2015. They were fighting against one another for power instead of working together for the common good of the people. Even the regime in power was dictatorial in that it imprisoned the elected

Members of Parliament of the Opposition Party. I represented the major political parties with the different rivers that I knew since my childhood time in my small hometown and made them fight one another to reflect the politics of the country at that time. I could not openly discuss my political views at the time for fear of being persecuted, targeted or banned from entering Ethiopia.

In many Westminster-style parliamentary systems of government, the loyal opposition indicates that the non-governing parties oppose the actions of the sitting cabinet while remaining loyal to the formal source(s) of the government's power, such as the monarch or constitution.

Come and visit us, Rediet Hotel, Butajira.

CHAPTER 9

Bright Butajira –
Future Battersea Town
or Boston City

Long ago, in the year 1989, when some of my Eritrean uni friends in Asmara asked me where I was from, I used to tell them, "I am from Butajira, a little sleepy village in the Southern Peoples' Administrative Region". They had never heard about this small town with its magnificent treasure – Zebidar. However, the present reality is far from how I described Butajira town in 1989. Things have immensely changed for good over the last three decades.

BUTAJIRA is explosively growing in every aspect imaginable. The people are grateful with the Local, Regional as well as the Federal Government systems for the direction of the economic development. Can you believe this? In the small town where I was born and grew up as a shepherd, shoe polisher and kolo seller, I became a total stranger travelling to my hometown with my family from the UK after fifteen years.

We took off from Addis Ababa to Butajira around noon and arrived in Butajira roughly around four in the afternoon. The town has completely changed and I asked pedestrians (people who were

Bemnet Kindergarten, Butajira.

walking on the sides of the street) to show me where my home is. "Where is Ato (meaning 'Mister') Tadesse Ergicho's home?"

Luckily, people knew who my father was and we were kindly directed. (We needed a tour guide to visit my own hometown.) My father was a famous district judge who worked for more than thirty-five years in a judicial role in the government. **One thing so special about him was every month he would buy a pack of 12 BIC pens and distribute them to the lucky children to promote education in the community at that time. He has a community spirit and used to advise people to be law-abiding.**

There was NOTHING like 'BUSINESS AS USUAL IN BUTAJIRA'. Everyone was busy working towards the economic development of the town in particular, and our country in general. Busy bees buzzing – their motto seemed, "Think Global and Act Local!" Well done, Butajira! Well done, ETHIOPIA!

The Tertiary Industry (Service Sector) in Butajira (the segment of the economy that provides services to its consumers. It includes a wide range of businesses such as financial institutions, schools and restaurants) has boosted far beyond expectations. There are three hospitals, several health clinics and pharmacies, two colleges and High Schools, Primary Schools and Kindergartens, factories of various types, big hotels and numerous high quality restaurants.

Speaking of kindergartens, I met and talked to the headteacher of Bemnet Kindergarten, Mrs Emebet Tadesse, and I was pleasantly surprised by the wealth of knowledge she had about children's education in connection with special educational needs which was not given much attention when I was in my Primary as well as Secondary Schools. She said, "Children have endless potential and we will do our best to cater for them in their academics, differentiating those who need more support." Keep up the good work you started on children and I would like to congratulate you and your team for earning "Zebidar's Educational Award (ZEA)" Celebrating Excellence in Education.

At the present, the focus with both local and foreign investors seems to be towards Manufacturing Industries and making Butajira an Industrial Zone. Gash (is a title) Abera with his flour factory, the Turkish Textile Industry, Ethiopia's First Herbicide Factory and the Rat Factory (the first of its type in Eastern Africa to produce cutting edge drugs/medicines) are the ABCs of what is going on around Butajira and beyond. It is a great start . . . I see Butajira town emerging as Battersea Town in London, or Boston – the largest city in New England and the capital of Massachusetts. For my dreams – the sky is the limit!

Blessings:

- *May God Mighty bless and give divine directions to our political and business leaders.*
- *May God Almighty bless the people and town of Butajira and beyond.*
- *May God Sovereign visit our beautiful land, ETHIOPIA.*

Practice Point:

- Have you ever thought of linking your hometown in your country of origin with the town or city you are living abroad?
- Have you also ever thought of linking schools and hospitals abroad with the schools and hospitals in Ethiopia for experience sharing?

CHAPTER 10

ABYSSINIA CLOSE

ABYSSINIA CLOSE is a name given to a road in South West London. You will find it on Northcote Road next to the famous pub called Northcote Records. However, did you know that Abyssinia was Ethiopia's old name?

Few countries in the world possess such wealth and variety of ancient legends and fascinating attractions as ETHIOPIA. The land-locked country of 1,235,000 square kilometres (47,833 square miles) is twice the size of France and shares borders with Djibouti, Eritrea, Kenya, Somalia and the Sudan. Ethiopia's outlets to the sea are at Massawa and Assab in Eritrea, and Djibouti port, in the Republic of Djibouti. (4)

Ethiopia is credited with establishing the green, yellow and red colours that have come to symbolise African independence and unity. Ethiopia is the oldest African state in history. The colours became known as Pan African colours. The three equal horizontal bands of green (top), yellow (middle) and red at the (bottom). The green represents hope and the fertility of the land, yellow symbolises justice and harmony and the red stands for sacrifice and heroism in the defence of the land.

Since Ethiopia is the oldest country that has never been colonised, the three colours of the flag were so often appropriated by other

African countries upon their independence that they became known as Pan African colours. On October 11th, 1897, a year after Ethiopia defended itself from Italian aggression at the Battle of Adwa, Emperor Menelik II, authorised the creation of a flag containing a rectangular tri-colour from top to bottom: red, yellow, and green. Later, the Ethiopian flag had its own process of getting the present form and shape.

Escaping from the story of flag, let me cast a light upon my journey of getting a job in the Ministry of Foreign Affairs of Ethiopia to defend my country's flag and National Interests at home and abroad as a diplomat – there were sixty-three students for one post of Third Secretary position in the Ministry. The composition of the competitors was among four batch of graduates in the previous years and I recall it was a fierce job competition.

Abyssinia Close.

We had a written examination on what should be the foreign policy objectives of Ethiopia towards neighbouring countries in Africa, Europe, America and Asia. The second question, I could not remember it very clearly. But I guess it was something to do with national interest. I wrote twelve pages of substance with the green brain I had at the time. I stood number one and was shortlisted with another fourteen competitors for interview at the time.

What made my written examination extraordinary was even before I went into the exam hall I declared in my heart, "I made the written examination in the name of Lord Jesus Christ and let it be Your Will for me to join the Ministry!" even before I saw the exam questions. My Lord is the Key for Success! *"I delight to do Your Will, O my God, Your Law is within my heart."* (Psalm 40:8)

I was shortlisted as number one for an interview and after a couple of weeks on the interview date, whilst I was directed to the interview hall I prayed, "I made this interview in the strongest name of Lord Jesus Christ. May Your Grace and Favour be upon me before my interviewers!" One question was about Islamic fundamentalism and how it would be a threat to Ethiopia in the future, the neighbouring countries, Africa and the whole wide world in general. The flow of information and knowledge from my brain was phenomenal. The General Directors of Africa, Europe and America, Asia and Australasia and International Organisations were nodding their heads as I was answering. So, to say, there were collisions of their heads as they were moving sideways in admiration.

They could not hide their appreciations of my personal and academic views and this is how the Lord of Lords, the King of Kings works in your life when you allow Him to do His Will. He has a perfect plan and purpose in my life. I could see God's Favour in both my written and interview examinations as the areas of the questions were subject areas where I had a wealth of knowledge and I was not short of answering their extended questions at the time.

"For I know the plans I have for you," declares the LORD, *"plans to prosper you and not to harm you, plans to give you hope and a future."* (Jeremiah 29:11)

I was making all the spiritual and mental readiness ahead of time to take the one vacancy the Ministry advertised in the month of March 1995. Nonetheless, before my employment, every time I was passing by the Ministry by bus number 31 from Sidist Kilo Addis Ababa university to Mexico Square to research "The Internal and External Sources of Employees in the Ministry of Mines and Energy" for my Public Personnel Administration course, I would stretch my hands and pray to God, "Lord let it be Your Will to secure me a place in this building". Passengers in the bus would look at me when I lifted up my hands but wonder what my mind was thinking – having conversations with the highest authority – GOD.

Well ahead of time in 1993, I had interviewed Ambassador Mohammed Ali on the topic of "Islamic Politics in North Africa and Middle East" when he was the General Director of Asia, Australasia and Middle East Directorate. That day after the interview Ambassador Fesseha Shawel Gebre invited me to a cafe later in the Ministry's lounge. But he was a junior member of staff at that time. Thank you, Ambassador Fesseha for your kind gesture and invitation on that day helping me to explore my would-be lounge.

In the Gergi Full Gospel Church, after I attended my salvation lessons given by Pastor Dr Yirdaw Tesema, when we were praying for an opening of job in the Ministry for me – Heaven was listening and the angels were comforting my heart. That time Pastor Yirdaw was an evangelist for the Full Gospel Church in Gergi. Thank you, Pastor Dr Yirdaw, for your heartfelt prayer which hit the target. We need more of those specific prayers of yours and the prayers of 1946 these days. Seventy-seven years ago, a great test on the efficacy of fasting and prayer took place in the city of San Diego.

In light of the physical, psychological and spiritual preparations there was one thing in particular which I needed to do. That was distancing myself from Dr Taye Woldesemayat who was the President of Ethiopian Teachers Association (ETA) with a piece of advice from someone who was working in the Foreign Office at that time. Dr Taye was an amazing professor who brought lots of phenomenal changes in the PSIR Department. He disliked the leaders of the then Ethiopian government saying, "They were liars!" and that he was openly criticising them cost him tremendously. He was sent to prison for a lifetime but served for several years and released.

He promised me that he would get in touch with the universities in the USA and find me a full scholarship. He said, "Merid, I do not want you to pursue your education like I did. I was collecting garbage to have my studies in the USA." He has a golden heart. However, if I kept on associating with him there would be no chance for me to get my dream job at the time. Hence, I stopped visiting him in his ETA office after my graduation.

Whilst he was teaching in the university, he was inviting several panellists from abroad like the late Canadian journalist Scott Young to talk on the Referendum of Quebec in light of the Referendum of Eritrea from Ethiopia. The similarities and differences of the two respective referendums – Quebec, Canada versus Eritrea, Ethiopia. Moreover, Professor Cornel West was also our guest lecturer, thanks to Dr Taye Woldesemayat's networking. Thank you, Dr Taye, for your sincerity and honesty in your life – respect!

Whenever the PSIR Department had guest lecturers, Dr Taye would give me the flyers to stick them on the boards, poles and trees so that other department students could also join in and enjoy the academic approaches to certain relevant discussions of our country, Ethiopia. It was a privilege to be one of his students.

Having said that, as you might be aware of the closure of all academic institutions in the UK for summer break around the end of July for about six weeks, it reminded me about the Palestine Ambassador in Ethiopia. I recall I had the following brief conversations with him. I met the Ambassador in the VIP Lounge of Bole, Addis Ababa International Airport waiting for his flight and his small follow-me cabin luggage right next to him. After we exchanged greetings, I asked him, "Your Excellency, are you going for a holiday?" He crouched down to my ears and replied, "There is no holiday for Palestinians. I am travelling for work."

Likewise, Ethiopian citizens won't have holidays until we stamp out the structured, complex, abject poverty and low level of economics in our country. Our people should see a decent life. We all need to be supportive of any micro or macro projects our country is undergoing by contributing finance and sharing of our knowledge whenever necessary.

The most important aspect of getting kids excited about volunteering is teaching them why? Does God care when we do something for someone else? Yes, God chose that we would live in community with one another. Volunteering is basically a component of what it means to be a human. And Jesus said that the two most important commandments are to love God and our neighbours.

Furthermore, encouraging volunteer work in Ethiopia could be beneficial to the people who are volunteering as well as the community. Feeling of a sense of purpose and fulfilment can be something very powerful. If you volunteer for a cause you care for and are passionate about, this will add extreme value to your life and allow you to use your skills for good. You will be also helping your community.

Below is a list of potential volunteering in different areas:

- Environmental Volunteer Work.
- Volunteering with Animals.
- Social Impact Volunteer Work (Children and Youth NGOs, Education & Teaching, Community Development, Women's Empowerment).
- Volunteering in Health Care and Holistic Centres (Health Care, Holistic Centres).
- Tourism Related Volunteer Jobs (Hostel/Guest House Administration, Digital Marketing and Web Development).

CHAPTER 11

THE GOD OF ZEBIDAR

"I lift up my eyes to the mountains— where does my help come from? My help comes from the LORD, the Maker of heaven and earth." (Psalm 121:1 – 2)

In the Spring of 1988, a heavily loaded Isuzu lorry was involved in an accident due to its faulty brake whilst the driver was driving it on the steep road of Dirama on its way to Butajira from Kela. First, the driver had tried his best to hold the brake and stop the lorry. Unfortunately, the lorry was uncontrollable and continued accelerating backwards down the steep hill with the driver trying to adjust the wheels along the road. Eventually, it turned four times before it came to its normal position unloading everything in it. All the passengers who were on the lorry received heavy or light injuries, except me who did not get a scratch as I prayed, "God, save me", sensing the terrible danger coming ahead. On the other hand, our friend who lost her life said, "Good-bye to us and the nearby farmers who were ploughing the land" right before the lorry turned over on all its sides.

"The tongue has the power of life and death, and those who love it will eat its fruit." (Proverbs18:21)

I was found on the tilled soil of a farm where the softness was better than over-the-top luxury of a seven-star hotel bedroom in Burj Al Arab Dubai. My instant prayer was heard in Heaven and God sent an army of angels to pick me up and take me away from the danger site. You might think I was tossed away onto the farm when the lorry turned over four times. No, absolutely not! I was carried away by angels of light. Glory to the Highest to Him forever and more.

The above is a true testimony of what happened on Saturday 9th April 1988 (Eve of Ethiopian Easter, Sunday 10th 1980 Ethiopian Calendar) around thirty-five years ago is a memory that stays fresh in my mind when I think of God's Love, Mercy and Divine Protection. I do not deserve it, but God is too good for those who sincerely ask Him in prayers.

In August 2016, when I was in my hometown of Butajira, I surprisingly bumped into Mrs Genet Taye who was with me in that lorry accident and reminded me, **"We are living EXTRA YEARS because of God's Grace." Yes, EXTRA YEARS and UNDESERVED BLESSINGS especially for me who was not worthy if it was not for His Mercy.** In God's time, the two of us who got God's favour met and praised Him for the most astounding and wondrous thing He had done for us.

God, My Heavenly Father, is always good. Abigail, my eldest daughter, once told me, "Daddy, if God didn't save you in that car accident, we (Joanna and I) would not be alive today." She also said, "Thank you so much for being the most amazing father to me and Joanna and may God continue to bless you in your life." She understood not only that children are gifts from God but also that He cares and saves those who believe in Him. She is my Pearl and the Apple of God's Eyes! God has an amazing plan over the lives of Abigail and Joanna. God is good all the time. Amen.

On the other hand, my Crystal Diamond and Miraculous youngest daughter, Joanna, discerned with her spiritual insights that all passengers could have been saved if my prayer was for everyone who was in that lorry. I recall, my big brother Sileshi saying exactly the same thing years back even before Joanna was born. Nonetheless, I did not pray for all and I prayed for myself and the Lord proved He was/is a God who answers prayers.

But lately my mind was racing with the idea of "How could my all-inclusive-prayer save all others especially when one said, 'Good-bye!'?". I know this is the first time I am disclosing this information to be public knowledge just in case it could be a lesson. I always kept it in the dark and never told anybody. The only other person who heard this "Good-bye!" word from the victim was Mrs Genet Taye who was with me at that moment. The deceased was sitting in the middle of us. RIP!

"I am the Lord, the God of all mankind. Is anything too hard for me? (Jeremiah 32:27)

The above implies no –nothing is impossible for the Lord if we are asking according to His will, with unwavering faith and trying our best with God's help to live a holy life. In another instance, Jesus replied, *"What is impossible with man is possible with God."* (Luke 18:27) proving God can do anything He wanted. He is omnipotent!

My big brother Sileshi preached the gospel to me when he came for his vacation from the Technology Faculty, Amist Kilo Addis Ababa University. He read me a verse from the bible "***For God so loved the world that he gave his one and only Son, that whoever believes in him shall not perish but have eternal life.***" (John 3:16) and invited me to receive the Lord Jesus Christ as my

Personal Saviour. I refused. I was a stony-hearted young man at that time. An additional verse he shared with me was *"I am the way and the truth and the life. No one comes to the Father except through me"* (John 14:6).

Sileshi cared to give testimony about the Lord Jesus Christ to me but he could not make me believe in Him. He could not control that! Only God can change people's hearts. Later on, my belief in the Lord Jesus Christ brings in some changes in my life. My big brother put the seed of life in me in the late 1980s which resulted in changing several lives in the UK and beyond. If you, or members of your family or friends, care to, you can consider Sileshi Tadesse Ergicho as your model. You will witness the changes in your own life and I would like to read the book you will publish about your impacts and as to who became a positive influence or life-changer for you.

However, God has His own timing, I came to His Kingdom in 1989 somewhat reluctantly when I was in Asmara University. *"Even before he made the world, God loved us and chose us in Christ to be holy and without fault in his eyes."* (Ephesians 1:4) Now I am established and rooted in the Lord Jesus Christ – the Alpha and the Omega of my spiritual life. He is the author and the finisher of my faith.

In a related topic, about forty years ago, my younger brother Sebesibe told me that he wanted to go to God and sit down with Him. *"Behold, I stand at the door and knock. If anyone hears my voice and opens the door, I will come in to him and eat with him, and he with me."* (Revelation 3:20) . . . *If anyone hears my voice* . . . Could it be a toddler? Could it be a teenager? Could it be an adult? It could be anyone. I think my younger brother heard Jesus' voice and opened the door of his heart at a young age. That explains why he has a heart closer to God.

I also say that each day Christ still stands at the door of your heart and knocks; do you open the door each day? Does He sit at your table, does He join you in your work, in your reading, in your watching, in your talking, in your listening? He wants to, He wants to share everything you have, all you are and He wants you to share all He is and all He will bless you with.

But how do we do that? Firstly, we do it intentionally; we decide that we want to . . . Do you really, do you? Jesus stands and intentionally knocks because He wants to come in. He wants to speak with us, but I fear the sad reality is, we do not often want to speak with Him, we do not intentionally open the door and spend time with Him listening and sharing.

So often we wonder why God does not do incredible things through His people, His church, as He has in the past? The answer is, His people, His church are not intent on seeking Him and serving Him, we say we are, but we open other doors instead, and the noise from them drowns out the knocking . . . or if we hear it faintly, we decide we are too busy, maybe we will open the door at another time, but it is not convenient right now. (5)

Once a wife kept on bothering her husband to go to the cinema and enjoy a movie with her. There was nothing wrong with that as he had done it several times before, but he told her he wanted to have a devotional prayer on that particular day. She insisted that he should go with her and he finally gave in to her request. They went to the cinema and at the counter he bought three tickets instead of two. She wondered why he'd bought an extra one and asked, "Why did you buy three tickets when we were two?" He answered, "I wanted God to sit down with us and watch the movie as I planned that particular time for my prayer to converse and connect with him. Let He connect with us by watching the movie." Will He?

"After the Lord Jesus had spoken to them, he was taken up into heaven and he sat at the right hand of God." (Mark 16:19)

This idea of living with God seriously came to my mind in my mid-forties. I have matured enough to go for God's way now as I had been through rough and hard roads because of my poor choices in life. Am I really matured? Not yet! I am still in the process of sanctification and I am not in any rush to go to Heaven as I need to accomplish my earthly duties before leaving Earth. BIBLE could stand for B – Basic, I – Instruction, B – Before, L – Leaving and E – Earth? I better believe in and say, *"I can do all this through Christ who gives me strength."* (Philippians 4:13).

The statistics of percentages for the following words show a divine connection of my brothers if you give a consecutive number to the English alphabets as A = 1, B = 2, C = 3 and so on.

- KNOWLEDGE = 96%
- HARD WORK = 98%
- ATTITUDE = 100%
- LOVE OF GOD = 101%

By the way, my three brothers are devout Christians who love God – They got 101%! God blessed them all. They live in Nashville, Tennessee.

As to me, "The Spirit of the Lord is on me, because he has anointed me to proclaim good news to the poor. He has sent me to proclaim freedom for the prisoners and recovery of sight for the blind, to set the oppressed free, to proclaim the year of the Lord's favour." (Luke 4:17 -19) I speak blessings over your life – peace, joy and love be yours for eternity.

I was in the evangelisation ministry under my church, Kensington Temple, at Notting Hill Gate, in London. I love doing it with my team at different chosen spots throughout London. It is phenomenal to see how God works! The last couple of years, I am attending church services with my brothers and sisters in Carshalton Evangelical Church every Sunday and the love of God is among us. My family and I moved home to Carshalton and God gave me a new community of believers.

I did evangelisation solely by myself, carrying tracts, praying and walking in the streets and distributing the gospel material at hand for those who volunteered to take one. I tell them that I will see them in Heaven one day when it is time. They would give me a smile, collect the tract and go – such happy moments! Do they read it? That will be God's part as providing His word is mine. Partnership with Jesus, the King of kings and the Lord of lords. Jesus is my Light and my Salvation and I am His Ambassador.

One day I told Abigail if someone asks me a kind of question like, "Looking back in your life, was there anything which you would regret for not doing it or something you wish you have

Leafleting Christian Literatures.

done but did not accomplish?" I told her it would be that I did not spread the good news that Jesus is the Lord, the King of Kings, Lord of Lords as much as I wanted to do it.

Then, she said, "Daddy, do it now so that you won't regret later in life." Tomorrow is not promised. She is right – I needed to do it now, so for that matter I bought a mega loud speaker to make sure everyone on the streets of London and its outskirts will hear me out loud and clear about the Gospel – the Good News from God. Jesus is the LORD! He died for ALL. THINK – Did anyone die for you so that you could live? No one did. ASK – Will there be anyone who is willing to die for you?

The word "gospel" means good news. It is **the news about who Jesus Christ is, what He has done, and how that changes everything for all of us**. The gospel, or the good news about Jesus, is the best and most important news you will ever hear. Briefly, the Great Commission is a concept that has been used to support the missionary activities of many Christian denominations. The Great Commission refers to several passages in the Gospel of Matthew, where Jesus Christ urges his apostles to make "disciples of all the nations" and "baptise" them. God has given us the task of telling everyone what he is doing. We are Christ's representatives. God uses us to persuade men and women to drop their differences and enter into God's work of making things right between them.

"We are therefore Christ's ambassadors, as though God were making his appeal through us. We implore you on Christ's behalf: Be reconciled to God." (2 Corinthians 5:20)

I am hunting people to Christianity in this land of God – the United Kingdom. In the school where I work, my colleague Jackie Berry started to run a club called "Christian Union" for Sixth

Formers (College Students) to assemble, pray, discuss the Bible and different aspects of Christian life. We meet every Monday, Tuesday and Thursday during lunch breaks from 12.40pm – 13.15pm. Members of staff who are attending the club are – Mrs Rosemary Osode, Pastor Hyacinth Lowe, Mrs Esther Omar, Mrs Mini Philips, Ms Nicola and myself. Sometimes the turnover for the Club could reach up to thirty-eight students.

CHAPTER 12

GOD IS IMMANENT

The immanence of God means that He is knowable, perceivable or graspable. For example, Jesus Christ is God incarnate (in the flesh) and therefore He was immanent in the first century among those who knew Him, perceived of Him, experienced Him with one or more of their five senses. However, nowadays we perceive and grasp Him through His wonderful creations "*The heavens declare the glory of God; the skies proclaim the work of his hands*" (Psalm 19:1) and through the spirit He sent us – Holy Spirit. What are the fruits of Holy Spirit? *"But the fruit of the Spirit is love, joy, peace, forbearance, kindness, goodness, faithfulness, gentleness and self-control. Against such things there is no law.* (Galatians 5:22 – 23)

When I decided to return to the UK for good from the States, I was shopping for some clothes in Burlington Mall in Maryland. As pure luck, I met the owner of the mall. He was an old man from India. I always remember what he said to me. He said, "Son, you do not decide your place of residence – the Master does!" He was right. In our conversations, this old businessman told me that he was one of the top three wealthy businessmen in India.

His friends' wealth rocketed in their own country, India, through the years. His wealth did not increase as much as he wanted in his investment in America at that time. But he was not sad either. He accepted the Master's choice of place for him. There is one famous saying which I saw on a poster. It read as, "Like a tree, we each must find a place to grow and branch out." I did not know who the author was for this popular quote in Ethiopia.

He mentioned to me the only thing he would ever regret was that he was not allowed to bring his eldest daughter to the US when he moved as an investor as she was over eighteen. Those kind of immigration laws which are not considering a family's sentimental values are everywhere on the planet.

Let me tell you my part of the story with the Home Office in the UK. By the time I left for the US from the UK, I was officially married to my wife who was a British citizen and Abigail was only one year old. At that time, nobody was allowed to marry in the UK even if someone had found their right partners. You have to pass through certain rigorous procedures like getting an approval of marriage from the Home Office before booking your marriage in the Registry Office of the Council. It was a very strict criteria as everyone has to fulfil the requirement for fear of bogus marriage. Could that be the reason why many people are not making commitments to get married in the UK at the present?

Putting strict standards may not be the right thing to do in some aspects of social and spiritual lives. That might be the reason for a knock-on effect on dwindling future marriages. Research shows that the number of marriages had declined in the UK for several years. The number of marriages has halved since 1970, from over 400,000 a year to just over 200,000 a year now. One reason could be a likely consequence of increasing numbers of men and women delaying marriage, or couples choosing to live together rather than marry, either as a precursor to marriage or as an alternative.

The Certificate of Approval (COA) was introduced by the Home Office. This immigration document serves as permission to get married or form a civil partnership in the UK and is used in lieu of traditional fiancée or visit for marriage entry clearance issued by British Consulates abroad. So, I had the COA and married in the Borough of Wandsworth Register Office. My wife and I were married according to the law at that time.

Then, I talked to one senior immigration judge about the legality of living with my young family in the UK. He advised me that I needed to leave the country and come back with Entry Clearance or Marriage Visa from the UK Consulates abroad. He further added that I needed to undo my diplomatic status and come to the UK as an ordinary citizen. I thank this senior immigration judge for his pieces of advice because I did not want to go through a complicated immigration process as a former diplomat.

I was aware of so many causes of tragic family separation because the immigration laws demand that someone who was an alien and married to a British national still needs to get her/his Entry Clearance from the British Consulates abroad. That was what I did in the British Consulate in New York, USA. I travelled from Washington, DC to New York British Consulate on the 14th of July 2007. After the officer looked into my application he said, "Sir, were you a diplomat in the UK?" I replied, "Yes, Sir!" Next, he said, "May you please be seated for at least half an hour until we process your Entry Clearance?" Spouse/CP of B Teshome was stamped on my ordinary Ethiopian passport. Done! I was granted in less than thirty minutes. God's Grace and Favour!

As I was celebrating my speedy marriage visa to come and live in the UK with my family, a white Scottish woman with her two children and a white American husband from New Jersey were advised to come back after three days to collect the Entry Clearance. She was not happy with the appointment of coming back after three days. It was like a football game – when one team celebrates its win the other team moans with its unfortunate defeat. I was not happy for the Scottish lady that she did not receive a fast-track service like me. I completely depended on God in the success of my application and probably she did not.

As happy as I was thanking the officer and collecting my documents and passport, I planned to go to the Empire State Building's top floor to celebrate my win and get closer to the skies where my God lives from eternity to eternity and cry out to Him, "Hallelujah! Thank You, God!" Is my voice clear to Your Majesty from the Empire State Building top floor? Can Your Excellency hear me?

"Oh, yes, it is very clear. You did not even need to talk. I could hear you as I am in your heart!" said the LORD. Anyway, His Majesty allowed me to be jubilant and when I was thinking of going to the building, God was thinking ahead of me doing something special. *". . . and who has extended his good favour to me before the king and his advisers and all the king's powerful officials. Because the hand of the LORD my God was on me . . ."* (Ezra 7:28)

I arrived at the Empire State Building. There was a long queue as there were several hundreds of international visitors from different countries lining up to visit this tallest building on the planet at that time. I saw a beautiful young lady who was working in the Empire State Building and the uniform she wore made her more attractive. I gave her a big smile. She gave me back twice as big as mine and started to come over where I was lining up.

We greeted each other affectionately with hugs and kisses even though it was our first meeting. She outrightly told me that I was her VIP guest and advised me to follow her up. I did exactly as she told me. She is from Eritrea and her name was Messeret Tekle, my angel of light from the Empire State Building. She got me a special lanyard to put around my neck and took me to the VIP Express Pass with red carpet to shoot to the top floor of the building. I was completely thrilled. Who was I to be treated like a king? I did not make any payment for entrance as God has already paid it for me through Messi's discretion.

Behold! There was more to come – more surprises from God to me as we were ascending that tall building to the 102nd floor. She said, "Tonight and as long as you are finishing your tour in New York, you will be my guest and stay in my apartment with my son and me. I have enough room for you." I did not know what to do or what to say. Was I dreaming? No, I was not! The Lord my God was with me wherever I went. God is immanent!

I said to God, "I am crazy and too much in love with You for who You are! I cannot live without You!" I wanted to fly in the blue skies of New York down to the seashores singing and praising Him on the top of my voice. People should know about Your ever-loving mercy and care. God knew I liked surprises. He is Omnipotent – all powerful. He has all-encompassing power. He is Omniscient – all knowing. He sees and hears everything. He is Omnibenevolent – He is all good and all loving. He cares for all His creations. He cares for you.

God is Immanent – belief that God is at work in the world and "He is with us", for example performing miracles – Jesus was an example of this as I mentioned in the first paragraph above. He died for our sins and on the third day He has risen. He is Transcendent – He is beyond space and time, not controlled or limited by either. He is Impersonal – He is beyond understanding. We may know more about Him by reading the Bible – the Living Word of God. Like what He did for me on my way to Hawassa, Ethiopia for my first job hunt in 1994. He has done it again on the 14th of July 2007 in the United States of America in New York. God is everywhere. He blessed me with His peace, joy, love, goodness and grace. He will bless you, too.

After I had my ninety minutes roaming around the building, looking through the binoculars and visiting the gift shop, etc, I told my dear Messi that I would come back on our appointment time in the evening and left the building. So, I was touring the different places in New York until she finished her work for the day. I went to her office to meet her in time and off we went to Brooklyn to her apartment. There I met her twelve-year-old son who surprised me with his level of maturity as we were chatting in the evening after dinner was served. His name was Noah and he shared with me the following great story.

He said that a long time ago there was this man who had wealth. One day, he planned to buy the best and fatty bull for his family for the Ethiopian New Year holiday, September 11. He put his cash in his pocket and set off to the market. On his way, some people from his village asked him where he was going early in the morning. He told them about his intention of buying the best and fatty bull from the market. They told him that the price of a bull was very expensive and sky-rocketing. He assured them as long as he had the money there would be no worries. Take it easy, men!

In the crowded open market when he was choosing one bull over another, the pick-pockets stole all his cash. He found one bull he liked and sent his hand into his pocket only to find out that all his money had gone. Disappointed and heart-broken he set off his home. On his way home, the same people who asked him where he was going in the morning asked him again where he was up to then. He said, "If God permits, I am on my way home." *"When pride comes, then comes disgrace, but with humility comes wisdom."* (Proverbs 11:2) Don't ever be proud of what you had, rather learn to say, "If God wills, I will do this or that . . ." without being arrogant.

Thank you, Messi and Noah for your unreserved hospitality during my stay with you in New York! May God bless you for eternity! His way is different for those who believe in Him. *"For my thoughts are not your thoughts, neither are your ways my ways,"* *declares the LORD.* (Isaiah 55:8)

CHAPTER 13

APRIL – Grand Thanksgiving Month

As I wrote earlier in chapter 11, God miraculously saved me from the car accident on Saturday, the 9th of April 1988 right after I prayed, "God, save me!" That is why I celebrate the month of April as my Grand Thanksgiving Month (GTM) in my life. It was a rebirth of me with mission by the most powerful authority – God.

It thrills me that I was born on the day of Ethiopian Christmas – January 7th and my christening name is Tekleyesus (literally meaning the plant of Jesus or who follows and checks his integrity in light of the LORD). I also wonder if there was any divine connection about my date of birth and my christening name. To date I do not have any insights to share.

However, I was reluctant to accomplish the mission of my rebirth on the Eve of Ethiopian Easter – to speak about the Lord Jesus Christ to everyone whom I met as His Ambassador on duty. I need to proactively spread the Good News for the ignorant as well as those who did not get a chance to hear about it if there are any as it is my number one priority in the affairs of God's Kingdom. That is one of the principal purposes of my life on this beautiful big earth.

On the 6th of April 2023, nearly thirty-five years after, the Holy Spirit awakened me from my spiritual retardation or death. As I was holding the big Cross with my right hand and praying for myself in the middle of the congregation in Carshalton Evangelical Church, West Street, Surrey on Good Friday on Reflections at The Cross, God was speaking to me that I did not fulfil His Mission on earth.

In connection with listening to the small and subtle voices of God, I knew a saint who explained it to me a long time ago. Her name is Mrs Tigist Kassahun Demeke (Mimicho) and she lives in Nashville, Tennessee, USA. In the year 2006, when I was in Nashville, she told me about an opening of our spiritual ears – ears which are active and ready to hear from God. I never heard anything like that before in my Christian life. Many times, I heard about spiritual eyes or spiritual eyes of our hearts when I attended church programmes. I always kept her message in my heart and longed enough to have one. It is my greatest pleasure to be a prayer partner with Mimicho that Glorious God blessed me with the fear of Him and learning His Living Words from the Bible. We recorded our audio messages, shared and reflected on them. We worked and grew up in the love of God. My sincere and fervent prayer to you, Tigist and Tsegab, is for God to bless you with eternal peace, joy and love.

Pastor Keith Waters, my Pastor at the Carshalton Evangelical Church, emailed me the part of the Bible which I will be reading for the Good Friday Programme. It was on Mark 15:6 –15. But I did not know how and why I read one extra verse. Could there be any spiritual reason not yet revealed or was it a simple mistake? I will wait from the LORD in this as many other unanswered prayers. Below are the verses I shared to our Good Friday gathering.

⁶ Now it was the custom at the festival to release a prisoner whom the people requested. ⁷ A man called Barabbas was in prison with the

insurrectionists who had committed murder in the uprising. ⁸ The
crowd came up and asked Pilate to do for them what he usually did.

⁹ "Do you want me to release to you the king of the Jews?" asked
Pilate, ¹⁰ knowing it was out of self-interest that the chief priests
had handed Jesus over to him. ¹¹ But the chief priests stirred up the
crowd to have Pilate release Barabbas instead.

¹² "What shall I do, then, with the one you call the king of the
Jews?" Pilate asked them.

¹³ "Crucify him!" they shouted.

¹⁴ "Why? What crime has he committed?" asked Pilate.

But they shouted all the louder, "Crucify him!"

¹⁵ Wanting to satisfy the crowd, Pilate released Barabbas to them.
He had Jesus flogged, and handed him over to be crucified. ¹⁶ The
soldiers led Jesus away into the palace (that is, the Praetorium) and
called together the whole company of soldiers.

I read my verses loud enough that the congregation could hear
me clearly. As I read, the Holy Spirit brought this thought to my
immediate attention, "Back in time, you were one of those people
who were shouting out 'Crucify him!' so that you need to repent."
It was a very clear message and I immediately repented – I have too
many sins to be forgiven and He had removed every single one of
them from my life. I am free! Not only that I glorified Him in my
heart to the highest and praised Him for eternity, I also let Him
preside in my heart and over my life. Moreover, I sang the following
song in my heart silently.

I have decided to follow Jesus;
I have decided to follow Jesus;
I have decided to follow Jesus;
No turning back, no turning back.

Though none go with me, I still will follow;
Though none go with me, I still will follow;
Though none go with me, I still will follow;
No turning back, no turning back.

The world behind me, the cross before me;
The world behind me, the cross before me;
The world behind me, the cross before me;
No turning back, no turning back.

Then, one of the Christian ladies came behind me and took over the big cross from my hand. I sat down on the chair still thinking about the voice and reiterating exactly what God said to me. Let me wind up our 'Reflections at The Cross' church programme with the song we sang at the end of the programme.

Song – Were you there when they crucified my Lord?
Were you there when they crucified my Lord?
Were you there when they crucified my Lord?
Oh, sometimes it causes me to tremble, tremble, tremble.
Were you there when they crucified my Lord?
Were you there when they nailed him to the tree?
Were you there when they nailed him to the tree?
Oh, sometimes it causes me to tremble, tremble, tremble.
Were you there when they nailed him to the tree?
Were you there when they laid him in the tomb?
Were you there when they laid him in the tomb?
Oh, sometimes it causes me to tremble, tremble, tremble.
Were you there when they laid him in the tomb?
Were you there when God raised him from the dead?
Were you there when God raised him from the dead?

Oh, sometimes it causes me to tremble, tremble, tremble.
Were you there when God raised him from the dead?
Benediction

About listening to God's voices, I would like to share Andrew Wommack's witness. He wrote, "I once was planning a trip to Costa Rica, a place I had been before, and was excited to be returning to. Yet, as I prayed about it, I lost my desire to go. Instead, I actually felt dread about going. The first thing I did when that happened was make sure I was really seeking the Lord with my whole heart. While on a road trip, I spent seventeen hours praying in tongues, and the more I got my mind stayed on the Lord, the less I wanted to go back to Costa Rica. On the strength of that alone, I cancelled the trip."

Furthermore, he added, "When the people of Costa Rica asked why, all I could tell them was I didn't want to go. That was hard to do, and I'm not sure they understood. **The plane I had booked my flight on crashed on take-off from Mexico City, killing all 169 persons onboard.** The Lord warned me of that and saved my life, not by saying, "Don't go to Costa Rica," but, by communicating to my spirit and taking away my desire to go. That is the dominant way the Lord speaks to us, and we often miss that kind of communication."

The following story which I modified a bit and did not know who the author was stirs my heart and reminds me what my Lord Jesus Christ has done for me on the cross. I ask, "Did I fully understand His deep, unconditional, incorruptible and eternal love He gave me for free?" Did you?

A widowed mom leaves her house and goes to fetch water, leaving her only child asleep. On her return, she found a large crowd around her burning house. On the inside, her son is about to die in the fire. Throwing her bowl of water on herself and on the floor desperately crying, she wants to get into the burning house to look for her son. Everyone keeps saying, "You are going to die too, fire is very great."

Escaping from their hands, she enters the fire and wrapped her son in a wet blanket. The child, tight against her breast, was not touched by the fire. Mummy comes out severely burnt and was narrowly saved; thanks to the care of the hospital, but she lived with scars and was unrecognisable. Many years passed. The child under the guidance of his selfless mother, completed his studies.

Later he worked hard in a legal firm as a successful lawyer and also won a big prize on a Euromillions lottery. He paid back all his student loan and bought a villa and luxury cars. He was also appointed as a government minister and he organised a party at his villa on his appointment, and invited all the dignitaries of the city and his friends.

While they were in full party, noises were heard at the door of the entrance to the villa. The son was forced to go and resolve the situation. He found that the security officers were preventing his mother from joining the party. Faced with this situation in front of his guests, he tenderly said to his mother: "Please, Mom, I would be ashamed to have you appear before my friends. We can discuss later." And in secret, he ordered the security services to throw out his mother because of her scars.

What inspires you in this story? This woman in the story represents the Lord Jesus Christ who sacrificed himself for you and I. Today, right now what place do you give him in your heart? Is He the King of kings and the Lord of lords in your heart? It is He who has received the scars because of yours and my sins. Have you received Him as your Lord and Saviour in your heart? If not, please pray the following prayer with me – **Lord Jesus, I believe you died for me and that God Almighty raised you from the dead. Please forgive all my sins. I choose to turn away from them now and I ask you to come into my heart and life as my Lord and Saviour.**

For we are to God the pleasing aroma of Christ among those who are being saved and those who are perishing. (2 Corinthians 2:15)

I was enveloped by the vivid, sparkling treasures of spring. The scent of bluebells was flung like wafts of perfume into the air. Do you smell something afresh in the air other than the flowers' smells? The aroma of my Thanksgiving to the Prince of Peace, King Jesus has been rising up in the beautiful blue skies filling the air with the most wonderful and extraordinary fragrance. My Heavenly Father, DADDY, deserves MORE and MORE . . . Glory be to the HIGHEST to Him who sustained my breath against all the odds of life such serious diseases and infirmities like Coronavirus.

I have a friend who ws miraculously survived Covid 19. He is so meek, kind-hearted and his generosity knows no bound when it comes to helping others. "*Blessed are the meek, for they will inherit the earth.*" (Matthew 5:5) Meekness is essentially an attitude or quality of heart whereby a person is willing to accept and submit without resistance to the will and desire of God. Thus, the main point about the meek is not their self-control, but rather their absolute faith and trust in God. Hence, to be meek means to always turn to God for help, for direction, for training and for the sheer joy of this blessing.

Ten Strategies for Cultivating Meekness

---

1. Moderate your expectations of others.
2. Find joy in evidences of God's grace.
3. Remember how much you have been forgiven.
4. Take time before you form judgments.
5. Make friends with meek people.
6. Take pleasure in the joys of others.
7. Discern God's hand in the work of your enemies.
8. Walk daily in fellowship with Jesus.
9. Anticipate all that God has promised.
10. Ask God to give you meekness.

Source: Open Bible by Colin Smith, Founder and Teaching Pastor.

My family and I are in good health because *WE ARE COVERED BY THE PRECIOUS BLOOD OF LORD JESUS CHRIST. MOREOVER, THIS ALL-POWERFUL NAME AND NAME ABOVE ALL NAMES PROTECTS US FROM ANY GREAT AND UNTIMELY DANGER.*

> *Follow God's example, therefore, as dearly loved children and walk in the way of love, just as Christ loved us and gave himself up for us as a fragrant offering and sacrifice to God.* (Ephesians 5:1-2)

God created Zebidar marvellous and beautiful in every way. The magnificent trees that lay across ZEBIDAR – Chains of Mountains of Butajira flung their branches up to the sun and framed the deep blue sky. ***ZEBIDAR is Thanksgiving Mountains.*** It gives pleasure to the people of Butajira. It's a prestigious gift to Ethiopia by Sovereign and Supreme God. Parts of the grounds of Zebidar is painted in yellow gorse and natural ponds. What a beauty!

There, in the middle of the most breath-taking meadows, stands a relatively tall man. He makes out to be around 5ft 11 and half-inches and showcases a well-built body. The creases in his forehead suggest he's around 50 years old. *He stood stretching his arms wide-open, praising, singing and worshipping God.*

The man, once a shepherd himself, says, *"Glory to You – the Prince of Peace – Jesus!"*

The Chains of Mountains echoed back saying, *"Glory to You – the Prince of Peace – Jesus!"* Next, he says, *"Glory to You – the Creator of the universe."* The Chains of Mountains echo back once again. At last, *"Glory to You – the Spirit of the Living God Who dwells in my heart,"* says the man and the mountains. Do mountains have hearts you may wonder?

I adore You! I revere You! I liload You! now and ever and unto ages of ages. AMEN.

Note:
liload - is a made-up word coined by my eldest daughter, Abigail. It meant **li - like**; **lo - love**; and **ad - adore**. She argues one of the emotion words by itself is not enough to express one's love to God.

Even in her eighties, my mum was giving her testimonies about the LORD to another old woman in one of my visits to Ethiopia. I knew she is a woman of prayer – three times a day. Morning, noon and evening. I pray to God to give me her passion and spirit of prayers to others in my life. She is an astounding evangelist who is happy to share what is best in her life with others.

One day in my childhood as my mum and I were walking to Mekicho where my grandmother used to live, a young boy came smiling and he exchanged greetings with my mum. She told me that she was praying for him to quit smoking and he honestly did.

One thing which surprised me was that even he did not know that she was praying for him. This is a wonderful grace which all Christians need to aspire to have. Are you that kind of person?

This one is one of her most fascinating prayers – to pray for dirty places so that they could be properly utilised in time. Land is a scarce resource everywhere but sometimes we see them not properly utilised and handled. Who did pray for a dirty and desolate place in their lives? I never heard and never read any book with this kind of content so far. Perhaps, my book will be the first book ever written with material revealing this secret of prayer about filthy places.

As we walk, my mum uplifted her hands to the skies and prayed for the dirty place. I recall I was in my Elementary School at the time. The very spot where she prayed for its favour was the first place where a big building was built in Butajira for the first time. What a prayerful mum I had! She is a mega-blessing to every single thing in my life including my own very existence. I knew the spirit of prayer my mum had is transcending into me. I prayed for three different dirty and abandoned places in London. Guess what? Big buildings are constructed on those places which I prayed for. You may wonder what is so exciting about it, even without your prayers skyscrapers could have been built. The least I knew I had fast-tracked it!

CHAPTER 14

Thank you – United Kingdom

My deepest gratitude to the people and the different respective governments of the United Kingdom which run the country since its formation. The good seeds you had planted in the past benefited me and made me curious to make a little difference in the area where I am working – teaching children and young adults. Furthermore, I am grateful, deeply grateful to the nurses and doctors who work in the National Health Service (NHS) in general and to those who work in the Wrythe Green Surgery, Carshalton specially to Sister Angela Farringdon who treated me tirelessly with the best of her professional knowledge as well as Ms Heidi Dieckman, a Health Care Assistant who has been greatly helpful, and the Falcon Road Medical Centre, Battersea for their support in the betterment of my health from the emergency and planned surgical wounds I have received.

The political maturity of the political parties namely Labour, Liberal Democrats, Conservatives and others, the respect and love among the people of this nation is astounding. The compassion and the kindness they show to other people who came to their country because they are humans is unimaginable. Once more, I would like to say thank you so much to the generous people and the fair government of the UK.

As far as my personal observation is concerned, football, rugby, cricket, tennis, socialising in pubs and abiding by the law are a few of the vital passions in people's lives in the UK. The people enjoy football as a major sport, socialise valuing the community, celebrating multicultural diversity in schools with respect and tolerance with individual liberty. Besides, they always wanted to observe the rule of law when they are trying to resolve potential or real difficult situations and outstanding problems. These excellent assets and social values ought to be learnt by some countries which fundamentally lack them.

It does not mean that there are no small problems at all and the country is perfect in every way. There is no country without a problem! Problems of every sort exist everywhere on the globe, But the question is how do we resolve it? Considering my own individual life, to write a few things about what I encountered in the past twenty-two years I would say they were very negligible or insignificant compared with the blessings I got by living in the United Kingdom. The UK is my transiting home before I go to the New Jerusalem.

Once I had bladder surgery and wanted to walk outside of home as a physical exercise. Hence, I was walking slowly like a tortoise and that got the attention of the neighbours where I was walking. They called the police as they were suspicious of my slow walk – probably they thought I was carefully moving, scrutinising and plotting something disastrous in the neighbourhood. On another occasion, after another surgery, I could tell my slow walking was attracting unnecessary attention from an old man who approached and asked me why I was walking very slowly.

I told him that I had had surgery recently and was recovering slowly from it. He said that I was lucky to be treated by white doctors. I just ignored him and kept on walking as it was not a fruitful conversation. Actually, the surgeon who operated on me was a black doctor. No hard feelings whatsoever as we are all humans and bound to make mistakes in our lives. I forgave him for his wrong and perverted personal views. His views would not represent the views of other wonderful people of this great nation. Henceforth, I have real admiration for the society's level of consciousness and I wished every community was positively cooperating with the law enforcement unit, community policing and neighbourhood watch groups.

Another incident was when I was walking inside a park where there was a children's playground, in my heart I wished my daughters were with me in the park at that moment. Next, I saw a police car with sirens and thought of them, how busy they were doing their best in bringing peace and stability in the city of London. Behold! They were parking not far away from the park I was walking. I saw three tall policemen jumping out of the police car and coming towards the park and I did not notice any illegal activity going on around the area. I wondered what had brought them into this peaceful environment. Funnily enough, then they made a left turn and were coming towards me. "Wow, these policemen did not have enough work to do which could keep them busy." I changed my previously held ideas about them being busy enforcing the law but did not blame them – they were trying to do their work.

They had stopped me and told me according to the description they had received that I was in the public's interest to be examined. They asked my name and my address. I told them my details. After I cooperated with what they needed I asked them why they had stopped me. They explained that they were informed by the public that there was something suspicious about me. Respect! No big deal. Good-bye! I took their badge numbers to report to the Metropolitan Police but did not waste my time as they fully explained their reasons fully and clearly. If it was an abuse of authority, I could have challenged them. But, it was not!

I wondered why incidents of these types come to me though. Could that be because I am black? No, I do not believe in that analysis. London is a very diversified city which is genuinely boosted with multi-culturalism. So is Croydon, the area where I work. In light of the park incident in Clapham, it could be just a paranoid parent or someone who had some psychological or mental health problem had called them because she/he envisaged something dangerous or uncomfortable. Whatever the case, the policemen were doing their work to the best of their ability and knowledge, to the best interests of the common good. Those were my own personal views in connection with the experiences I had been through since April 13, 2001, the day on which my foot touched this beautiful land of God, the United Kingdom.

However, sometimes when you are trying to do something good, you could end up in atrocities with your own life. The following is a true story about a gentleman from Ethiopia who was living in London. His immigration status was pending as he came from Saudi Arabia which was a safe third country. He left his wife and three children in Saudi Arabia to seek asylum. The Home Office considers a ‹safe third country› to be a country of which the individual seeking asylum is not a national or a citizen; and in which the person's life or liberty is not threatened by reason of race, religion, nationality, membership of a particular social group, or political opinion.

One sunny and bright day as he was walking, he saw a little girl crying, standing on a stone wall outside of her home. He thought the little girl was in danger of falling and approached and got her down to the ground. Her mum who had been watching what was going on from inside her home through the glass window had dialled 999, an emergency call to the police, and this gentleman was arrested on suspicion of trying to abduct the little girl. In the court hearing the gentleman explained that he had lifted the little child up from the wall and put her down to the ground safely when he saw her in a difficult situation of balancing herself.

Anyone could tell that she was in fear of falling to the ground. The mum thought he was a paedophile. However, after his lawyers explained to the child's mum that he had done it in good faith for a good cause – to save her child from falling to the ground, the mum dropped her case and thanked him for his good deed. But that good act cost him a lot – he has to be deported to Saudi Arabia. Contrarily, he should have been rewarded for getting the little girl to the ground safely. But it did not happen. The odds of challenging life in the eyes of the law . . . Whatever it will cost you, do not hesitate to do good to others in times of their need.

I like the good act of the king who saved his guest of honour from embarrassment. Once a king invited a scientist to dinner at his palace in honour of his scientific discovery. After dinner was served it was time for tea and the scientist was pouring his tea into a saucer to drink from it. The noblemen who were seated there along with the King were about to burst into laughter for the unusual way the scientist was drinking his tea. When the king noticed that he put on a stern face and as a result they all suppressed their laughter. That was a kingly act to save his guest of honour from embarrassment and discomfort. What is your kingly act to save someone from some kind of uneasiness in people's lives? Everybody has got one – think and act towards achieving that goal in your life.

On a separate note, I met the late Queen Elizabeth II a couple of times and on the those occasions she allowed me to have a brief conversation with Her Highness. She was a great mind reader and deliberately asked me, "Young man, you got something to say?"

On my way to Buckingham Palace to meet the Queen.

The first one was at Buckingham Palace. I answered, "Yes, Your Highness, I was wondering when you may have your second visit to Ethiopia. I knew you had a state visit before in the 1960 during Emperor Haile Selassie's reign and you had visited the Nile basin and also the city of Gondar where my wife came from." On her state visit to Ethiopia, she returned Emperor Tewodros' royal cap and seal to Emperor Haile Selassie. She said, "I hope I would like to visit your country one day." Her smile was kind and royal. Unfortunately, her hope of visiting Ethiopia once more did not happen.

I am glad I was doing my job as a diplomat and later as a public diplomat to encourage people to travel to my country. That will help the travel and tourism industries to grow financially and expand the sectors to several tourist destinations. In fact, every time I had that chance of talking to people, I always told them that there are lots of cultures, historical places and natural sceneries to visit in Ethiopia. Among the very best are Simien Mountains National

Park, Fasil Ghebbi Castles, Gondar Region, 18th century Gondar Atatami Kidus Mikael built by Emperor Dawit III, Lalibela Rock-Hewn Churches, the Fortified Historic Town of Harar Jugol, Tiya Archaeological Sites in Soddo Region on the way to my hometown – Butajira, the Imperial City of Axum, Konso Cultural Landscape, Lower Valley of the Awash, Lower Valley of the Omo and Arbaminch.

I knew my country's image was tarnished by civil wars and famine on several occasions. Ethiopia was not most Europeans, Americans and Asians' tourist destination, even if it had lots of tourist attraction sites. It was overshadowed by the negative publicities which did not focus on the good things the country could boast. However, Ethiopia is a mosaic of so many different cultures, music and as a result various cultural and traditional dances and foods. You won't regret it – go and visit ETHIOPIA!

Another opportunity to talk with Her Majesty was when she invited the diplomatic community to her Windsor Castle for a buffet dinner. I would love to talk to her as much as I could, for, I did respect her as she was "The Defender of the Faith" and a wonderful person to talk to. This time I talked to her about the Ethiopian Prince whose graveyard was in Windsor Castle. I asked her if Her Majesty's Government was willing to return his remains to Ethiopia in an official ceremony. She agreed to it but I knew she would have to convince her government first. However, this request was raised recently in 2023 by family members of Prince Alemayehu, and Buckingham Palace responded that it would be impossible to attempt to recover the Prince's corpse as it will disturb other members of Royal families who had been buried in the surrounding area. However, I do believe an official request should be repeatedly made by the Ethiopian Government towards this achievement.

On the other five occasions I was with other invited guests – two Trooping the Colour Ceremonial Events and three Tea Parties where the Queen was in attendance.

If you happened to walk around Hyde Park closer to the Royal Albert Hall, you will find a statue of Lord Robert Napier on horseback where it is encrypted "Magdala". That is a historical town where the war between Ethiopia and Britain took place. The young Prince came as a war captive when the Ethiopian King, King Tewodros, made war with Queen Victoria's modern army led by General Robert Napier. The King did not want to be arrested so he took his own life with the pistol Queen Victoria sent him as a gift.

The widowed Empress Tiruwork and the young heir of Tewodros, Alemayehu, were also to be taken to England. However, *Empress Tiruwork died* on the journey to the coast and was buried in Tigrai province of Ethiopia. Prince Alemayehu made the journey alone but grew increasingly lonely in imposed exile in England. Prince Alemayehu was only seven years old when his father committed suicide. Later the young prince, Prince Alemayehu, became increasingly lonely, unhappy and depressed during his time in the UK. In 1879, the prince died of illness at the age of 19. He was buried near St George's Chapel, Windsor Castle with a funeral plaque placed to his memory by Queen Victoria. (6)

I had this rare opportunity to get access to read a manuscript in the Humanities Department of Imperial College by one of the professors there. I read the story that King Tewodros had proposed marriage to Queen Victoria. Could it be in the best interests of modernising Ethiopia with science and technological advancement that Great Britain had achieved at that time? If Queen Victoria had accepted the King's marriage proposal, we could have been cousins with the British people. He was the one who unified Ethiopia to the present shape. Historians believed that he was a man ahead of his time. He was our hero and he still is a hero in the hearts of millions of Ethiopians.

On the other hand, Emperor Haile Sillasie was the King of a country which has never been colonised. Thus, Ethiopia was the only country from Africa which was the founding nation of the League of Nations which later became the United Nations.

Ethiopia's international image was phenomenal though it had its own domestic problems during the emperor's time. Ethiopia was also the founding member of the Organisation of African Unity (OAU) which later became African Unity (AU).

Three leaders of countries randomly received letters of interviews from the highest authority – God. The three leaders were the 3rd Israeli Prime Minister David Ben-Gurion, President Gamal Abdel Nasser of Egypt, and the Ethiopian Emperor, King Haile Sellasie. God was at the centre hall of the building where there were three other separate rooms connected to it by doors.

First the PM of Israel was called and he went into the hall to have his interview. He greeted and thanked God Almighty for the opportunity to be seen by Him. God asked, "What is your ultimate wish during your time of premiership?" He answered, "God, I wanted to see Israel surrounded by its peaceful neighbours." Are neighbouring countries (Lebanon, Syria, Jordan, Egypt and Palestinian territories) surrounding Israel friendly?

God said, "Well, this could happen but it may not be whilst you are in power." Thank You, Almighty God – thank you for the hope. He left.

Next, was the Egyptian President. He greeted and thanked for the opportunity to be interviewed. God enquired, "President Gamal, what would be your ultimate wish during your presidency?" He replied, "I want to see an independent Palestine country."

Egyptians always assume they had a regional leadership role in North African (Maghrib) countries and the Middle East.

God said, "This could happen sometime in the future. However, it may not be when you are still in power." He thanked Almighty God and he left. Palestine is not a country yet but is recognised as a sovereign state by 138 countries out of 193 United Nations member states as of 31st July 2019.

The last interviewee was the emperor. His Majesty went into the interview hall. Like the other two who had already had their interviews, he greeted and thanked for the opportunity presented. God asked, "What is your ultimate wish during your time in power?" The emperor answered, "My ultimate wish is to see my people eating three meals a day . . ." Before the emperor finished his ultimate wish, God started to sob. Terrified and shocked by what happened the King of Ethiopia asked, "God, Almighty – what happened? What happened?" In a whispering, shaking and broken voice.

God said, "Your ultimate wish won't happen let alone in your time but also in my time."

SAD. SAD. SAD.

God lives from eternity to eternity and there will be no way that Ethiopia will be self-sufficient in terms of feeding its people. An old Ethiopian gentleman who used to live in London told me the above story as I was invited to his home for dinner. I was working at the Embassy of Ethiopia at that time. I was in tears in the train going back home from Preston, London Borough of Brent to Roehampton, Wandsworth where I used to live. Why is it that the country and the people of Ethiopia live in treacherous poverty? Was it merely a joke or was there something else which was holding the country back? Even now in 2023, Ethiopia is one of the hungriest countries in the world. The list includes countries like Afghanistan,

Nigeria, Somalia, South Sudan and Yemen. The Global Food Crisis /
World Food Programme has projected Ethiopia to be one of those
counties in the world which encounters food insecurity.

The extent and severity of poverty have different causes and
manifestations in the rural and urban areas of Ethiopia. For the vast
majority of the people living in rural areas, the causes of poverty
include lack of income, pervasive disease, malnutrition and lack
of decent health care, schooling and clean drinkable water. On
the other hand, the multi-faceted manifestations of urban poverty
are a fast-growing population of street children, homelessness,
prostitution, beggary, a rising army of unemployed, overcrowding
and congested living conditions that serve as breeding grounds for
diseases and crime.

Poverty as being a problem with not one cause but many, it is
really wiser to identify the poverty problems the country has on its
own merit. That is why, at the end of a very long productive life,
Charles Darwin wrote, "Looking back, I think it was more difficult
to identify the problems than to solve them." Henceforth, poverty
is a commonly known concept often identified with such human
deprivation as starvation, malnutrition and homelessness.

The above political jokes break my heart and I always believe
that the Ethiopian people need to work together despite their
political differences to throw the abject and structural poverty the
country is in. That time for sure we will be at the end of the tunnel
seeing a glimmer of hope to come out of poverty and live a decent
life. Others did it so could we! Leave politics to the politicians
and focus on your own work. Use your legal and constitutional
rights to vote as an exercise of democracy to make changes in the
government.

**"Education is the most powerful weapon which you can use
to change the world."** This quote by Nelson Mandela is one of the

most famous sayings on the value of education. Education is what the Ethiopian people needed to change the present status quo of fighting each other – being in a vicious circle of civil war for the lust of power and money by the few political elites who are using the masses for unnecessary wars.

Ethiopians always pray – let us genuinely pray to God. That is good. Ethiopians need to walk and believe in God who is *"our ever-present help in trouble".* (Psalm 46:1) What we lacked is knowledge and wisdom. Knowledge is information of which someone is aware. Knowledge is also used to mean the confident understanding of a subject, potentially with the ability to use it for a specific purpose.

"My people are destroyed from lack of knowledge." Because you have rejected knowledge, I also reject you as my priests; because you have ignored the law of your God, I also will ignore your children." (Hosea 4:6)

Wisdom is the ability to make correct judgments and settled decisions. It is an intangible quality gained through our experiences in life. Wisdom, as in the Old Testament, is a God-given and God-centred discernment regarding the practical issues in life. Wisdom comes from prayer for God's help. God gives generously and without reproach (He does not want anyone to hesitate to come to Him). The Bible also tells us in James 3 that there are two types of wisdom: There is the wisdom of man that is "earthly, unspiritual, demonic" and full of "envy and selfish ambition". There is the wisdom of God, "the wisdom that comes from heaven, is first of all pure . . ."

An old woman crossing the veterinary College of Debre Zeit, Ethiopia saw how the vet doctors were looking after the donkeys in their sanctuary and she uttered, "Almighty God, I wish You made me a donkey." That was absurd! Wasn't it? I learned the vet doctors were from England who had volunteered to teach in Ethiopia. I could see lack of knowledge even in this true story of being jealous of a donkey. Why did the old woman wish to be a donkey to be treated well? Was it not easier for her to sincerely pray to God to find a way so that she could be treated much better than the donkeys as she was created in God's image and likeness.

We are in this problem of poverty partly because of what we are asking for from God. Instead of prayers of blessings, we say prayers of curse on ourselves. Then, we get what we prayed for or parallel to the words which came out of our mouth. Do you remember my friend saying, "Good bye!" to us when the lorry had faulty brakes on the hill and was involved in an accident? It is very unfortunate that sometimes we bring troubles to ourselves for not thinking positively and appropriately.

"But the things that come out of a person's mouth come from the heart, and these defile them." (Matthew 15:18)

Don't you see whatever enters the mouth goes into the stomach and then out of the body? But the things that come out of the mouth come from the heart and these make a man 'unclean'. For out of the heart come evil thoughts, murder, adultery, sexual immorality, theft, false testimony and slander.

"Ask and it will be given to you; seek and you will find; knock and the door will be opened to you." (Matthew 7:7)

This law of God is universally applicable wherever you live. After undertaking a mini-research on my students on their academic and behavioural traits, I prepared a small colourful dream card on which they could write one academic achievement they would like to see and the other blank space where they could write any behavioural challenges they had but wanted to improve on it. I got this general idea of a Dream Card from Dawit Dreams who is doing astonishing work in the transformation of people's lives in Ethiopia.

The reactions were unbelievable! Some of them came to me and told me that "Sir, living in Croydon we do not see any dream will ever come true. Someone could stab us on the back and we'd be dead. So, what dream are you talking about? We do not know what the future holds for us." The uncertainties of their lives were significant and they live in fear of dying. Actually, they did not realise that this self-generated fear is found in its acronym: F.E.A.R. or False Evidence Appearing Real. It appears real, even though it is a fear of the future and is not happening now. Therefore, it has no real substance, arising when the ego-self is threatened, which makes you cling to the known and familiar. Ceferino Benedicto Jr. has said that fear is nothing more than "False Evidence Appearing Real".

While others used the dream card and improved both in their academics and some behavioural issues as I expected, the worst scenario which was triggered by this dream card was when one of the students openly asked in the classroom, "Sir, what will you say if you see me as a homeless person on the street ten or fifteen years from now?" One thing I noticed though was even being born and living in a country of the largest economy won't save someone from poor imagination and negative perception of life. It is very unfortunate to see children live in fear of death and poverty in the UK. How could we tackle outstanding problems like these?

What goes around comes around. How was it possible this young boy's brain faculty was able to think something bad instead of something good? He was attracting bad future events in his own life. I reprimanded him – please speak something good, positive and work hard to see the fruits of your effort. "Do your best and God will do the rest!" The point is why was it the Ethiopian people were not able to live the decent life they deserve to live, get the attention, care and respect they needed? A fundamental change needed to occur, not only in the perception of the people but also in our many sayings which are filled with failure, negativity and bad motives and intentions in life. **Much effort is necessary to be successful in our lives – easier to say than practise.**

In regards to poverty, in May 2022, the Independent Food Aid Network (IFAN) surveyed 101 of its organisations representing **194 independent food banks** across 94 local authorities in England, Scotland and Wales. By the year 2022, around 2,173,158 people depended on food banks for their survival. Food banks are **community organisations that can help if you can't afford the food you need.** You'll usually need to get a referral to a food bank before you can access resources from them. How they work is non-perishable, in-date food is donated by the public at a range of places, such as schools, churches, and businesses, as well as supermarket collection points. It is then sorted into emergency food parcels by more than 28,000 volunteers, to be given to people in crisis.

Poverty has a global nature and inequality is increasing all around the world while the world is further globalising. Even the wealthiest nation has the largest gap between rich and poor compared to other developed nations. In many cases, international politics and various interests have led to a diversion of available resources from domestic needs to western markets. Historically, politics and power play by the elite leaders and rulers has increased poverty and dependency.

Eventually, after reading the introduction of this book, Abigail shouted out the name of the Prime Minister of the UK, "Rishi

Sunak! Rishi Sunak! Rishi Sunak!" checking whether I would react like my dad by getting my leather waist belt to whip her for calling the Prime Minister's name or not. Instead, I cheerfully joined in her chanting of calling out "Rishi Sunak!" and we burst into dad-daughter laughter.

I bless the holy name of God with all my heart. Yes, I will bless the Lord and not forget the glorious things He is doing for me including writing this memoir to the loving memory of my father, Tadesse Ergicho Fule Dendiso.

I also thank God for His grace (God's Riches At Christ's Expense), for His Mercy, for His Forgiveness, for His Protection, for His Guidance, for His Friendship, for His Peace, for His Unfailing Love and for being my Saviour.

God is good all the time and Jesus is the LORD.

Amen.

REFERENCES

1. Mohamed Amin, Duncan Willetts, Alastair Matheson, Journey Through ETHIOPIA, Cambrai Publishers International, Nairobi, 1997, page 10.
2. Dr Billy Graham, Answers To Life's Problems, GUIDANCE, INSPIRATION AND HOPE FOR THE CHALLENGES OF TODAY, World Book Publishing, Milton Keynes, England, 1988, pages 32 & 33.
3. Internet – Grace to you – Unleashing God's Truth, One Verse at a time "Can one who commits Suicide be Saved?"
4. Mohamed Amin, Duncan Willetts, Alastair Matheson, Journey Through ETHIOPIA, Op cit. page 10.
5. Pastor Keith Waters, West Street Evangelical Church, Carshalton, Notes, March 2023.
6. Matthies, Volker (2010). *The Siege of Magdala: The British Empire Against the Emperor of Ethiopia*. Princeton, New Jersey: Markus Weiner Publishers.

BIBLIOGRAPHY

Dr Billy Graham, Answers To Life's Problems, GUIDANCE, INSPIRATION AND HOPE FOR THE CHALLENGES OF TODAY, World Book Publishing, Milton Keynes, England, 1988.

Mind, Body and Spirit, Augustine of Hippo, First Edition Kindle, by Henry Chadwick.

Mohamed Amin, Duncan Willetts, Alastair Matheson, Journey Through ETHIOPIA, Cambrai Publishers International, Nairobi, 1997.

The Bible, The Living Word of God.

Email Address:

mergicho@yahoo.com

Please leave any comments you like in connection with the book entitled, 'The God of Zebidar'. I would like to hear from you.

www.ingramcontent.com/pod-product-compliance
Lightning Source LLC
Chambersburg PA
CBHW072013040426
42447CB00009B/1610